THE RIVER SEVERN

ALSO BY KEITH KISSACK

The River Wye. Terence Dalton Ltd.

THE RIVER SEVERN

by

KEITH KISSACK

TERENCE DALTON LIMITED
LAVENHAM . SUFFOLK

1982

Published by
TERENCE DALTON LIMITED

ISBN 0 86138 004 5

Text photoset in 11/12 pt. Baskerville

Printed in Great Britain at
The Lavenham Press Limited, Lavenham, Suffolk

Contents

Index of Illustrations

Acknowledgements

SO MUCH has been written about the Severn since the Romans reached it that any new book on the subject must be, in part, an anthology of what others have recorded. Wherever possible I have made acknowledgement in the text, and a list of most of the works I have used will be found in the Bibliography.

In consequence, this book is more a commemoration of the river as it was, than a guide to what is there now.

I am indebted to many people: to Mr S. D. Coates, Mr Andrew Helme, Mr David Williams of the Severn Valley Railway, Mr Alan Sockett, Dr Alan Jones and Mr O. Talog Davies for advice and help with the illustrations: to Mr A. M. Haigh and Mr A. S. Churchward of the Severn Trent Water Authority for information about the present administration of the river; and to Mr D. H. Jones for the trouble he has taken over the photographs. I am especially grateful to my wife and to Mr Derek Bayley for their criticism, suggestions and encouragement.

43106 crosses the Victoria Bridge at 13.30 from Bridgnorth on May 26th 1974.   *J. B. Hicks*

Introduction

1. The River.

THE *Oxford Dictionary of English Place-Names,* having traced the Severn back through Bede and Gildas to Tacitus, confesses that "the etymology of this ancient river name is not clear". There was no such diffidence in the twelfth century when Geoffrey of Monmouth supplied all the details of the drowning of Sabrina by a jealous step-mother, "whereby it cometh to pass that even unto this day the river in the British tongue is called Sabren, which by corruption in other speech is called Severn."

Giraldus, who mocked many of Geoffrey's pronouncements, accepted this one, and went on to explain how Sabren had become Hafren, the Welsh name by which its upper reaches were known. Hafren Forest still shrouds its descent from Plynlimon, and William Worcestre, writing in the fifteenth century, believed that it did not become the Severn until a few miles above Shrewsbury. The story of Sabrina was elaborated by later writers, from Drayton and Spenser to Milton and Swinburne, while John Keats was contemplating a poem on the subject during the last few months of what he called his "posthumous existence" in Italy.

If there were doubts over where the Severn began, there was also uncertainty as to where it became the Bristol Channel. Giraldus thought that it ended between Chepstow and the mouth of the Avon, and this is now accepted by the Severn Trent Water Authority, which gives it a length of two hundred and twenty miles, ten miles longer than the Thames. It provides England with a large part of its water, and in meagre compensation, receives the only river flowing from England into Wales, the small tributary, the Camlad.

The rainfall varies from an annual average of ninety inches near Plynlimon to about one quarter of that near Tewkesbury. But the flow of water is not dependent on rain alone. It is affected over much of its length by the huge variation in the tide at Chepstow, where a maximum of forty-eight feet is exceeded only on the Bay of Fundy* in Canada. This, coupled with the ever-narrowing channel, gives rise to one of the Severn's best known features, the Bore or Higre. Drayton, in the sixteenth century, dramatised the scene, describing in excited verse, how "it comes with hideous cry,

*Bay of Fundy divides Nova Scotia from New Brunswick where the tidal rise and fall amounts, at certain seasons, to 53 feet.

> And on the angry front the curled foam doth bring
> The billows gainst the flanks when fiercely it doth fling;
> Hurls up the slimy ooze, and makes the scaly brood
> Leap madding to the land affrighted from the flood,
> O'erturns the toiling barge"

and so on. A more scientific description was given by Sir Charles Blagden, Secretary of the Royal Society, in the late eighteenth century:

He was standing on Alney Island at Lower Parting, watching boats and dogs in the river downstream: "On a sudden, the boats and dogs are instantaneously raised up and thrown into violent agitation, and at the same time a vast wave or wall of water, reaching across the whole channel of the Severn, and dashing everywhere over its banks, is seen approaching with extreme rapidity. In a few moments it breaks violently against the point with a vast surge and prodigious noise; the wave is instantly divided by the shock, and each part rushing up its proper channel . . . is quickly out of sight."

There are some 255 bores each year, but only when the moon and the tides are suitable is it worth watching. The wave can reach a height of five feet and a speed of ten miles an hour, but the sort of melodrama Drayton described is rare. One of its side effects was to make the river as far as Tewkesbury, the highest point it reached, a public fishery. This was a characteristic of rivers that were both tidal and navigable, ensuring traditional fishing rights which were limited only by Act of Parliament, charter, or ownership of the bank.

The Severn has always suffered from flooding. The Romans, with typical thoroughness, seem to have built embankments to protect their forts at Forden and Caersws, but banks were never the complete answer, and most places on the valley floor accepted the inevitable. Occasionally, parishes close to the river, like Minsterworth and Arlingham, diverted church funds to maintain the flood walls, but with little permanent effect.

Sabrina by Peter Hollins,
Shrewsbury. *The Author*

2

Hollinshead described the great flood of 1484, "the Duke of Buckingham's Water," which contributed to his defeat and death: "Several persons were drowned in their beds, children in cradles swam about the fields, and beasts were drowned, even on the hills." In the same century, the Franciscans had eight feet of water in their friary at Shrewsbury, and when the Earl of Warwick was buried in the chancel of their church at Worcester, it was said that he would be drowned rather than buried.

In the flood of 1606, the levels between Bristol and Gloucester were covered to a great depth. A contemporary described how, "about nine in the morning, the sun being fairly and brightly spread, huge and mighty hills of water were seen . . . tumbling one over another . . . to the inexpressible astonishment and terror of the spectators . . . But so violent and swift were the huge waves, and they pursuing one another with such rapidity, that in less than five hours space most of the countries on the Severn's banks were laid under water, and many hundreds of men, women and children perished . . . Houses, barns, ricks of corn and hay, were all involved in the common ruin. Many who were rich in the morning were beggars before noon; and several perished in endeavouring to save their effects."

The heights of the floods of 1672, 1770 and 1795 were recorded on the walls of Worcester; and John Randall copied from an old house near the Abbey in Shrewsbury a plaque marking five feet of water and the words:

This plate is fixed to let you know
That Severn to this line did flow.
     February 11th, 1795."

This was probably the deepest and, certainly, the one which caused the most damage. The conditions which led to it, (almost identical with those before the flood of 1947), were described by Telford in March of that year: "This season has been severe beyond all precedent. The storm of Frost and Snow kept accumulating for two months, after which a very hasty thaw caused a greater inundation than has ever been known in England. Much injury has been done by the various rivers, and the Severn has not been behindhand; that and other collateral streams have demolished many bridges," including sixteen in Shropshire alone.

The nineteenth century, too, had its troubles; the Worcester Hailstorm in 1811; the year 1818, when a gale overturned the Worcester Mailcoach, the Severn flooded five times, and there was the longest drought in living memory; 1847, when the river rose eighteen and a half feet in five hours; and the flood of 1852, which did so much damage to Minsterworth church that the floor had to be raised by four feet. Appropriately, the church has fish carved on the capitals, and Christ walking on the water in the vestry window. What might

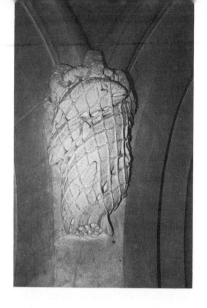

have proved the worst disaster of all was the tidal wave of 1883 which reached the railway at Woolaston and flooded the workings of the Severn tunnel, the men having to be rescued at great speed by moonlight.

Capital in Minsterworth Church. *The Author*

High water was a challenge to the railways, and the first train on the Severn Valley line, which left Worcester during the 1862 flood, was greeted by the band of the Bridgnorth Rifles playing "See the Conquering Hero comes" when it steamed safely into their station. Six years later, flooding at Caersws washed away the embankment, and the train from Newtown went over, killing the driver and fireman.

But not all river tragedies were due to flooding. Two naval officers and a small boy lost their lives, while boating at Tewkesbury, within four days of one another in 1818. And Sir John Wolryche died near Quatt when attempting to swim his horse across the river after an all-night celebration at Chelmarsh Races in 1723. The Reverend F. E. Witts confided disapprovingly to his diary, "There were three servants with him and some boatmen in a boat within forty yards when he was drowned. He was drunk, I fear." Drunkenness at Broseley was even more likely to lead to disaster, especially amongst boatmen, groping their way back to their barges late at night.

Ferries were another hazard. Eight people were drowned when returning to Sandhurst from Maisemore Feast in 1785 and, according to John Randall, twenty-eight lost their lives when crossing from the porcelain works at Coalport in 1799. Forty years later the Aust ferry foundered with all hands.

Such accidents led to the formation of the Severn Humane Society in 1786, "for the recovery of persons apparently dead from drowning." A complicated system of awards was agreed, depending on whether the rescued were alive or dead. £2 was divided amongst rescuers when a life was saved, though no one was to get more than ten shillings (50p). If the victim was dead the amounts were halved, and by 1802 the *Gloucester New Guide* was claiming that over three hundred people had been saved in the sixteen years since the Society was founded.

The Clywedog Dam and the Bryn Tail lead mine. ▶
The Author

The present policy of the river authorities is to protect urban areas and agricultural land by building flood defences and improving the channel. Caersws and Newtown have already been defended, and schemes are in hand for reducing the danger at Shrewsbury, Worcester, Gloucester and Tewkesbury. It is assumed that the river will overflow somewhere about once annually.

But such occurrences have not always been looked upon as disasters, and Defoe recorded the belief that, like the Nile, the Severn "impregnated the valleys, and when it overflows, leaves a virtue behind it peculiar to itself; and this, they say, is confirmed because all the country is so fruitful, wherever this river does overflow and its waters reach." Cooke, a hundred years later, agreed with this, pointing out that the Ham at Tewkesbury was so frequently enriched by flooding that manure was never needed.

Others who held the same opinion were suggesting that land, which was protected by embankments above Shrewsbury, was much less fertile than that which was exposed to flooding. They advocated flood-gates which could be opened in winter and closed in summer when there was a danger of crops being washed away. Telford, too, had considered the problem, and thought the answer would be reservoirs in Montgomeryshire, which would conserve the water during times of high rainfall, and release it when the river was too low for proper navigation. He made his proposals in *The Report on the Agriculture of Salop* in 1803, and in 1964 Llyn Clywedog was constructed above Llanidloes. It is a regulating reservoir, covering 615 acres, holding eleven thousand million gallons, held back by the highest mass of concrete in the kingdom, and designed to do exactly what Telford suggested at the beginning of the nineteenth century.

2. Transport

In the seventeenth century the Severn was navigable for one hundred and fifty-five miles below Welshpool. It was then, after the Meuse, the second busiest river in Europe. A contemporary member of Parliament likened it to "Veins in the Natural Body, which convey the Blood into all the Parts, whereby the whole is nourished and made useful." They were veins which were spared the obstruction of weirs, which did so much to hinder navigation on the neighbouring Wye. For centuries the Severn remained "The King's high stream," a free river with shipping lanes kept clear by the strength and extent of the tides; not only linking the riverside communities with each other, but the whole region to Bristol and thence to the rest of the world.

Only above Welshpool was the river not navigable, and in 1749, the vicar of Llanidloes, writing to London for a hundred Bibles, asked that they be put in panniers, "otherwise it may not be easy to have them carried into these parts." A year later, Captain William Owen, journeying from Llanidloes to London, travelled overland to Shrewsbury where he boarded a wherry in the morning, breakfasted at Atcham, drank tea at Bewdley, and arrived in Worcester at nine at night. Two days later he hired a horse to ride to Oxford. Communications above Welshpool were not eased until the first train, on what was to become the Cambrian Line, set out on its inaugural journey between Newtown and Llanidloes.

Below Welshpool, the boats which carried both passengers and goods, were barges and trows*. The barges, about fifty feet long, single masted with a square sail, could carry about fifty tons. The larger trows, some sixty feet long with main and, sometimes, mizzen masts and square and lateen sails, could carry up to eighty tons. They had internal keels, round bilges, and masts which could be lowered at bridges. This was achieved by fitting the mast into a box called a tabernacle, and hingeing it on a bolt at the bottom. It was secured when upright by an iron bar at the top of the box.

When sails could not be used, barges and trows were dragged by men, known as bow-hauliers, who were linked to a tow-rope by a harness which went round the chest and over the shoulder. The rope went to the top of the mast, and the Burghley map of Shrewsbury shows four men pulling a barge in this way in 1575. Celia Fiennes remarked on a similar scene at Worcester, boats being drawn "by strength of men, six or eight at a time." Telford called the system barbarous, slave-like and expensive; and John Fletcher of Madeley watched with horror, men bathed in sweat, harnessed like horses to their traces, and supporting themselves with one hand on the ground as they struggled slowly upstream. They differed from beasts, he thought, only in that horses had collars and pulled quietly, while the men laboured "with loud contention and horrible imprecations."

---

*A trow was adapted to meet the Severn's peculiarities (shifting sands, high tide, Bore etc.), In consequence it was shallow, with rounded bilges and a flat bottom, often sloping upwards in the middle to facilitate crossing sand banks. Trows using other rivers, such as the Wye, had local modifications.

The West Gate and Bridge, Gloucester, 1830. From *Picturesque Antiquities of the English Cities* by John Britton.

Brian Stevens

They were not popular, being feared as dangerous, untrustworthy and inefficient; but they resisted all attempts to replace them with horses. In 1831 they behaved so badly at Bewdley that the Riot Act had to be read and a detachment of Scots Greys called in to restore order. Boat owners operated a contract system, called "Mugging," to ensure that hauling was completed. It was in force on both Severn and Wye, and involved the acceptance of a mug of ale by the haulier, as a pledge that if he failed to complete the journey he would be liable to three months imprisonment. Inns where the agreements were made were called Mug Houses, and special mugs were occasionally produced for the purpose.

Commercial navigation has a long history. The sheriff of Shropshire hired a barge for half a mark, to take his wife from Bridgnorth to Gloucester in 1198; and Shrewsbury was using barges to import paving stone a hundred years later. Traffic increased over the centuries, and by 1756 there were 376 vessels owned by traders living between Welshpool and Gloucester. Trows by this time were worth about £300 when newly rigged; and a normal charge for carrying freight from Shrewsbury to Bristol was ten shillings a ton, or fifteen shillings (75p.) in the opposite direction.

A hundred years later, stage coaches and the turnpike system became a threat to river navigation. A few traditionalists, like John Cresset, deplored the trend, despising stage coaches as "effeminate to His Majesty's subjects . . . (making them) not able to endure Frost, Snow or Rain or to lodge in the fields . . . and hindering the Breed of Watermen who are the Nursery of Seaman, and the Bulwark of the Kingdom;" but their protests were ignored.

Diglis Weir, Worcester.   *The Author*

A partial answer to the turnpikes had been the construction of canals to link the river with the industrial Midlands. Telford and others had produced figures which indicated that a horse could draw five-eighths of a ton in a stage waggon, thirty tons in a barge on the river, and fifty tons on a canal. So the canal system began to develop at almost the same time as the turnpikes, only to reach its peak when tramroads, the precursors of the railways, were being introduced.

With the canals came weirs. Strata Marcella had owned one from the early days of that abbey, but Henry VI had appointed commissioners to ensure that they never obstructed the navigable stretches of the river. Four hundred years later new ones had been built at Worcester, Tewkesbury and Gloucester, and Randall pointed out that they made the river secondary to the canals, obstructed its free navigation, destroyed the advantages of tidal flow for upward-bound vessels, and seriously hindered the passage of fish.

Just as the canals affected the river, so did the turnpikes. The early ones were so bad that they were no real threat; the Reverend Richard Warner, floundering along a Shropshire turnpike in August, 1797, thought them "of all public ways the most abominable." But as the punctuality of the post became a matter of honour, the maintenance of the mail routes improved. Better roads meant more traffic, and more traffic demanded better bridges. Thomas Penson built them in Montgomeryshire, John Gwynne at Atcham and Shrewsbury, and Thomas Telford, "Pontifex Maximus" as Southey called him, most of the others.

Although bridges, like weirs, obstructed the free passage of masted boats, there were still, in mid-nineteenth century, some four thousand watermen and their families working on the Severn. But the building of tow paths, the introduction of horses and, after 1814, the success of the steam tugs between Gloucester and Worcester, began to affect their numbers. The first passenger-carrying steam packet, *The Sovereign*, blew up on her maiden voyage in 1821, but she was followed by others, small like the *Sabrina*, or capable of carrying three hundred passengers like the *Holt Castle.*

The Severn Valley Railway, with Sabrina appropriately in the middle of the splendid company seal, was opened in 1862, and was the final nail in the coffin.

Barges at Lydney.
S. D. Coates

Twenty years later Randall found not more than half a dozen barges operating above Stourport, and this in spite of the fact that it was still possible to send an iron grate from the makers at Coalbrookdale to Bristol for a mere sixpence, and with far less likelihood of it being damaged than if sent by rail.

Traditionally the last barge sank at Bridgnorth in 1895, bringing to a temporary close an enterprise which brought not only wealth and employment to a large area of the country, but provided the kingdom with trained seamen to man the boats, built from the timber growing along the banks. Only one trow, *The Spry*, which was built at Chepstow in 1894, seems to have survived. It is moored at Diglis Basin in Worcester and is being restored by volunteers. For the rest, the ribs and skeletons of barges and schooners, lining the Lydney waterside, are sad memorials of a great undertaking.

It was one which had been bedevilled by civic and commercial jealousy in its early days, in the same way that it was embarrassed by technical innovations in its last years. For although the river was nominally free, it was extremely difficult to prevent the larger towns trying to monopolise trade by exacting toll from boats from elsewhere. As early as 1308, the bailiffs of Worcester had been accused of seizing the boats of those who refused to pay them toll, and a hundred years later the Bewdley boatmen were alleged to be banding together to stop anyone passing, unless he hired a local boat at an outrageous charge.

This made nonsense of Parliament's declaration that the Severn was "common to all the King's liege people for carrying merchandise to and fro in trows, floats and drags." But the enthusiasm of each town to establish its own closed shop was equalled only by the fury with which they denounced the practice by others. Thus, in 1430, the traders of Tewkesbury were complaining that great multitudes of common people from the Forest of Dean, "in manner of war, as enemies of a strange country," were boarding their boats, looting them, and hewing the craft in pieces. In consequence no one dared to approach the Forest, "being wild of people and nigh adjoining to Wales." They specified eight trows plundered and their boatmen thrown overboard to drown. The object of all this ferocity was "to force them to hire boats from the said Welshmen for great sums of money, an evil example and a great impoverishment of a King's liege people."

Accusations continued to be bandied about; Bewdley complaining that, if their men did not come to the Worcester quays and pay toll, they were attacked by the citizens with stones and arrows; and Gloucester alleging that Bewdley had forced men carrying timber to that town to cut their boats in pieces, "otherwise they would have cut off their heads." Only a threat of government action united the towns, and a proposal in 1784 to make the river more navigable, by building a succession of locks, led to violent demonstrations on the quay at Worcester during a visit of George III, barge owners and trowmen alike shouting themselves hoarse in calling on the King to keep the river free.

Drought probably caused more trouble than flooding. Even in a normal summer the river was not always navigable, so that when the level rose, fleets of barges came down to Gloucester, unloaded, and then returned as quickly as possible. Telford claimed that in the last decade of the eighteenth century there were times when there was as little as a foot of water in parts of the river, and that in 1796, the year after the great flood, there were only two months when loaded barges could be brought downstream. In contrast, high water might make the bridges impassable: "A vessel may go up when the water is low . . . and may not be able to get back for days if the river rises." The solution, Telford's regulating reservoirs, did not appear until commercial navigation had almost ended.

3. Fish

The Severn supports almost every type of British freshwater fish, including barbel which were re-introduced in 1956. But none was more esteemed in early days than the lamprey. Camden observed that "Severn feeds such a number of River Lampreys that nature seems to have made a pond for them in that place, such as the Romans anciently invented in the height of their luxury."

They have been a favourite food of royalty for many centuries, and Henry III maintained his own weirs near Westbury where tenants of the manor paid "pridgavel", entitling them to take such fish from the river. They seem to have been surprisingly expensive. It cost Lord Berkeley £6: 7: 2 to send six of them to Edward III, and Lady Elizabeth Huntington, shopping in Gloucester in the same century, ran up the following bill:

```
24 lampreys   21/-
Baking 6 lampreys   4/-
Carrying them to Steventon   3/4
1 yard of canvas to carry them   6d
Salt for salting 18 lampreys   2d.
```

The corporation of Gloucester made a practice of sending lamprey pies to the royal family, and Richard Hempsted, the last prior of Llanthony Secunda, foreseeing the closure of his monastery and looking to his own future, sent a present of cheese, carp and baked lampreys to Henry VIII, shortly before the Dissolution.

Although there is still an inn called *The Lamprey* in Gloucester, the popularity of the fish has declined along with its numbers. Cooke's *Guide to Worcestershire,* at the beginning of the nineteenth century, found it "much esteemed by those who are accustomed to revel in the luxuries of epicurism," but warned visitors to remember how Henry I died.

Almost in the same category as the lamprey were salmon and allis shad. The latter, a particularly bony creature, is now no more popular than the lamprey, but salmon remain the most sought after of all fish, and the species on whose capture man has expended most effort and ingenuity. Lave nets, putchers, putt weirs, stop nets, long nets, thrusting spears, rods, drugs, poison and explosives have all been tried, in spite of frequent Acts of Parliament seeking to control their use and design.

The Act of 1778, replacing one of 1667, and applying to both Severn and Vyrnwy, laid down many restrictions, specifying the dimensions and mesh of nets, forbidding Sunday fishing, defining the close seasons, and outlawing the use of lime and Cocculus indicus. The latter, now known as Anamirta cocculus, was an East Indian plant whose poisonous berries were used in homoeopathic medicine and to poison fish. It is curious that such an obscure plant should have become so available as to warrant a special reference in the 1778 Act.

It is equally strange that the fullest prohibitions have usually been on the taking of the most numerous of all river creatures, elvers. From the reign of Elizabeth I until 1778 their capture was completely forbidden, but in that year it became lawful to catch them to eat, but not to sell. In spite of the penalties, the order seems to have been ignored in Gloucestershire, and in 1779 Rudder described how "the country people skim them up in great abundance, scour and boil them, and bring them to market as white as snow, where they usually sell at about two pence a pound." Even these rights were removed in 1873, but the furious opposition of Severnside fishermen led to the Elver Fishing Act, of three years later, which introduced close seasons. These in turn, were removed in 1935, and elvers are now, with whitebait, the only fish fry which may be freely caught for food.

Elvers were traditionally looked upon as an aphrodisiac. The extent of this belief locally could, presumably, be gauged by consulting the riverside parish registers to see whether baptisms were unusually high around Christmas. True or false, it was an additional hazard to the elver; but those which evade the fishermen after their three-year journey from the West Indies, have a few seasons of comparative peace before returning as eels to face the barrage of nets, basket traps, spears, sniggles and tongs waiting to destroy them, before they again brave the Atlantic to reach their birthplace and beget more elvers, 99.9 per cent of which will die before reaching these shores.

One other factor which affected fishing on the upper Severn was the building of the nineteenth century weirs. Salmon could surmount them in high water, but they were impassable to many other fish such as shadd, lamprey and flounders. This benefited all fishermen below Gloucester, but deprived people upstream of a significant part of their diet.

Today, commercial fishing has become less important and has given way to recreational angling for coarse fish. The practitioners of this immensely popular pastime, as individuals or members of angling clubs, now provide a large proportion of the regular visitors to the Severn.

The river was never considered picturesque, and was not, like the Wye, looked upon as one on which the eighteenth century man of taste might study the theories on beauty of the Reverend William Gilpin. Indeed, A. G. Bradley, writing in 1920, could affirm that "the Severn is not a sociable river . . . and has comparatively little truck with house-boats, pleasure boats, water picnics and all such traffic." In fifty years things have changed with a vengeance, and the Severn now has more of such traffic per mile than almost any other British river.

Fishing at Atcham.

With it have come the inevitable problems of bank erosion, obstruction of the channel, pollution and litter. This, in turn, has compelled the authorities to prefer marinas to bankside mooring. In so doing they have added a new and sometimes incongruous element to the Severn scene; and it is arguable that they have now gone as far as is prudent in the interests of sociability.

Thomas Habington, in the seventeenth century, called the Severn, "the bewtifull ornament and prodigal benefactor of our County." If he could see it today he would probably find it less beautiful, and far too prodigal of its favours.

4. The Land.

So much for the river. What of the people living near it? Geology and climatic change have decided its course and determined where its people should settle; and the strata of the rocks through which it passes are conveniently displayed on Sedbury cliffs. Equally appropriately the rock names, Ordovician and Silurian, commemorate the tribes which once inhabited the Severn countryside, their magnificent iron-age camps covering a longer continuous period of human habitation, and providing a more permanent memorial, than anything left by those who came after them.

Although a seventh century conference of bishops decided that the Severn divided the British from the English, and Giraldus agreed that it had been the boundary between England and Wales, it has never for long been a national frontier. Owen Glyn Dwr (Glendower) hoped to extend the Principality "up the Severn to Worcester North Gate," but the failure of his rebellion only served to make the Welsh the scapegoats for many of the river's later troubles. Occasionally, dioceses and hundreds have been bounded by it, and for short stretches it divides counties; but many parishes extend across it, and most attempts to establish permanent boundaries have failed. On the contrary, its many crossing places have made it an ineffective barrier, while features like the Ford of Montgomery have become recognised diplomatic meeting places.

It was certainly no barrier to the Roman armies when they entered the tribal areas and established Gloucester, Wroxeter, Forden Gaer and Caersws along a great part of its length. Nor did the width of its lower reaches prevent them using the Forest of Dean as an industrial reserve. Once peace was assured, Wroxeter became the tribal capital of the Cornovii, and Gloucester a colonia for retired veterans. At Lydney they left behind a temple to the Celtic god Nodens, and when the imperial armies had gone the princes of Powys returned to take over much of the old tribal territory.

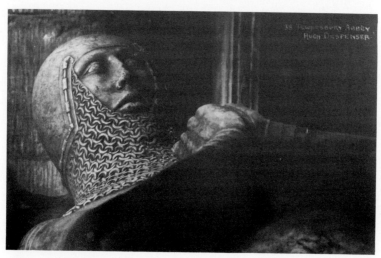

Hugh Despenser, Tewkesbury Abbey.

W. A. Call

But not for long, as Saxon invaders pushed them back to the upper Severn, where place-names like Leighton and Buttington mark the limits of the advance. They did not cross the river and Offa's Dyke, marking Mercia's western boundary, left it in Welsh hands as far as Llandrinio. Shropshire became the first of the Mercian shires to be named, but the Saxons suffered in turn from the most ruthless of invaders, the Vikings, who in 877 pitched their tents in the borough of Gloucester and then sailed upstream to sack Deerhurst. But Celtic, Roman, Saxon and Viking influences were all submerged in the eleventh century with the arrival of the great Norman families and the setting up of the Marcher lordships.

The new towns which they established, often based on a triple foundation of castle, priory and market, eventually evolved into the boroughs we know today. But in the beginning they were primitive and inhospitable settlements to which immigrants could only be attracted by privileges granted by the king. So the early March became the hunting ground of adventurers and mercenaries who could keep what they could capture and hold what they could rule. By mid-thirteenth century, Matthew Paris could write that "Wales was brought to naught . . . the land was unwillingly under the laws of the English . . . the harp was tuned to mourning."

The March, inevitably, became a danger zone to all concerned, not least the English kings. But the intrusion of the great royal holdings, like the Duchy of Lancaster and the earldoms of Shrewsbury, Worcester and Gloucester, reduced the power of the lesser lords, and prepared the way for their emasculation by Henry VIII. By 1360 the unknown cartographer of Gough's map was well aware of the importance of the Severn towns, and carefully distinguished their status by symbols. Thus, Bristol, Gloucester and Shrewsbury are shown as cities with crenellated walls, spires and houses; Bridgnorth and Worcester with spires and houses; and Tewkesbury with houses alone.

The Act of Union in 1536 set up six new counties and promoted the Council of the Marches to be the governing administrative body under the Privy Council. Its jurisdiction covered all the counties through which the Severn flowed, and, under active presidents like Bishop Rowland Lee, it did much to reduce the lawlessness which was rife. Amongst his many measures was one to regulate the ferries crossing the Severn estuary and to limit their sailing to the hours of daylight.

The new counties established by Henry VIII, together with the old ones, remained relatively undisturbed until 1974 when local government was reorganised. And although Powys was reborn, the rest were dismembered and amalgamated into units which were soon recognised to be historical and administrative nonsense.

5. Farm and Forest

Around the new Norman towns, but not on the Welsh uplands, a settled system of agriculture grew up, accompanied by the destruction of the forests. In the unaffected Celtic areas the old method of transhumance, the movement of flocks and families between summer and winter pastures, continued. Pennant, in the late eighteenth century, described the hafod or summer residence as a long low room with a hole at one end to let out the smoke. "Their furniture . . . stones and their beds . . . hay. Towards winter they descend to the hendref or old dwelling where they lead . . . a vacant life."

It was also a hard one, and a petition from Powys to Charles I in the early years of the Civil War underlined the plight of "many thousand families in the mountainous part of the country who, sowing little or noe corne at all, trust meerely to the sale of their cattle, wool and Welsh cottons for provisions of bread." The wool depended greatly on trade with Shrewsbury, whose monopoly was symbolised by the woolsack with which it decorated its tokens; and the cattle depended on the Welsh drovers whom Archbishop Williams of York likened to "the Spanish fleet of Wales which brings us what little gold and silver we have."

Husbandmen on the lower Severn had a more placid life, and Marshall, in the eighteenth century, found them "plain, frugal, painstaking, close and unintelligible." Their labourers were, similarly, "simple, inoffensive, unintelligent and slow;" but they were industrious, milkmaids for instance, "being at hard work from four o'clock until bedtime." Even so, they had a healthier life than industrial workers. At William Reynolds' iron works, each person had to be at his proper place from six in the morning until six at night, and absence or indolence meant a reduction in the weekly wage.

The happier side of country life can be seen in the marvellous paintings of Dixton Manor about 1730 in the Cheltenham Museum. The colourful lines of reapers, hay makers and Morris dancers, spread across the fields with military precision, are in cheerful contrast to the more mundane labours of the months, carved on the misericords in Ripple church.

Further north, Fuller had found Shropshire "a large and lovely county, generally fair and fruitful, affording grass, grain and all things necessary for man's maintenance, but chiefly abounding in natural commodities." Later reports to the Board of Agriculture tended to prefer the county's mineral wealth to the richness of its soil.

Thus Charles Hulbert in 1836 described Coalbrookdale as "the most extraordinary district in the world: the two banks . . . studded with Iron Works, Brick Works, Boat Building Establishments, Retail Stores, Inns and houses, perhaps 150 vessels on the river, actively employed or waiting for

Ironbridge by George Robertson (1788)   *Dr Alan Jones* ▶

cargoes, while hundreds and hundreds of busy mortals . . . enveloped in thickest smoke and incessant dust are cheerful and happy."

Charles Dibdin, the actor, had a very different opinion of the pleasures of living at Coalbrookdale. Overcome by the heat from the furnaces and the stench of sulphur, he likened the Gorge to hell, the Severn to the Styx, the toll-keeper on the bridge to Charon, while "the men and women might easily be mistaken for devils and furies, and the entrance of any one of those blazing caverns where they polish the cylinders for Tartarus."

If there were doubts about Shropshire, there were no such misgivings over Worcestershire and Gloucester. Here Cobbett found pasture of the richest kind, with great herds of Herefords, "certainly the finest and most beautiful of all horned cattle," mixed with fine flocks of Leicester sheep. He also found a pig in every cottage sty, "the infallible mark of a happy people."

In the early days of Severn agriculture, the most scientific and successful farmers had been the monks. Their monasteries acquired many privileges, and their foundations extended from Strata Marcella in the North to Llanthony Secunda in Gloucester. And because of their success and the extension of their lands, they became the most ruthless destroyers of the forests.

More than half of Shropshire was under forest law in the late twelfth century, but the activities of the monks were not the only reason for their destruction. The demand for timber for shipping, for charcoal in the forges, for bark in the tanneries, and for the materials of the timber-framed house, all played their part. Much of Dean has survived, as have remnants of Morfe and Wyre, but their former extent is best illustrated by the place-names commemorating every kind of wood: Hasfield (Hazel), Cressage (Oak), Awre (Alder), Purton (Pear), Willey (Willow) and Berkeley (Birch) are but a few; while Elmore on the lower Severn, lies in an area where elms were more useful than oak, because they lasted well in water and were preferred when building quays and boats.

6. Buildings

When the Civil War was over, most of the remaining castles were demolished, though a few, such as Powis and Berkeley, survived to be re-edified as country houses. Others, like Hanley, were replaced on a new site (Severn End); and for the next two hundred years great houses like Cound Hall, Loton Park, Attingham, Dudmaston and Elmore became the administrative centres of the countryside and the homes of those whom Habington likened to "the Cedars of our Shyre, flouryshinge above us in the Sunshyne of fortune, and in her stormes more subject to blastes." They were "the pretious dyamondes in the coronet of our County, gyvinge lyght to the inferiours howe to direct theyre lyfes." They provided the members of Parliament and the local magistrates; they replaced the monasteries as innovators in agriculture; they introduced new architectural fashions into houses and churches; and in their homes, local craftsmen learned fresh techniques of decoration and construction.

In towns and villages the timber-framed building continued to be built long after brick and stone had become available. *The New Inn* and Bishop Hooper's House in Gloucester were both built in the fifteenth century; but Ireland's Mansion at Shrewsbury, and Bishop Percy's House in Bridgnorth, arose in the late sixteenth, when country houses like Elmore and Naas had already been constructed in stone. Similarly, the Market Hall at Shrewsbury was being built of stone at about the same time (1600) that the citizens of Llanidloes were erecting theirs in wood.

Indeed, in the upper reaches above Newtown, farms, cottages and belfries continued to be built in traditional timber materials well into the eighteenth century. On the lower Severn brick took over more quickly, and one of the most attractive features of many riverside villages and towns is the mixture of black and white and Georgian brick which survives.

But it was the church which provided the greatest opportunity to the artists and craftsmen of the Severn valley. At Gloucester, Tewkesbury and Worcester the highest professional standards were set, and their influence percolated downwards to the parish churches which formed, not only the social and spiritual centres of the community, but art and craft galleries as well. They provided permanent exhibitions of artistry which the simplest labourer could wonder at and the humblest apprentice emulate. Metal and glass, stone and wood, furnished the English craftsman with the medium which his fellows in Italy found in oil and tempera. A great deal of the glass and many rood screens have gone, but our comparatively tranquil history has allowed much of the rest to survive. A short list might include the woodwork at Ripple and Melverley, the roofs at Llanidloes and Alberbury, the fonts at Holt and Slimbridge, the glass in St Mary's, Shrewsbury, and monuments at Wroxeter, Elmore and St Nicholas, Gloucester.

Bishop Percy's House, Bridgnorth.

Moreover, the parish church remains a living museum of social history, commemorating on its walls the piety and diligence of the clergy, the pride and public service of the gentry, the resignation of the widow and orphan, the fortitude of the husbandman and the mariner, and the valour of forgotten heroes from the fields of Waterloo and the Orange River. It may be, as Doctor Johnson said, that "in lapidary inscriptions a man is not on oath," but who could fail to be moved by Izaak Walton's farewell to his wife on the tablet in Worcester Cathedral, or the memorial at Slimbridge to the doctor who died with his young daughter after nursing her through a fatal illness?

Benefaction boards, darkened by time, high on the walls of the tower, recording charitable endowments for the old, the sick, the young, are evidence of practical benevolence and concern for the community. Nor can the visitor fail to notice the military history that lies behind the comparative length of the two casualty lists inscribed on the village War Memorial. And where else in England will one find a church which remembers so nobly the men of its regiment, as does St Chad's in Shrewsbury for the King's Shropshire Light Infantry? Here, even the bells have a martial ring:

"Success attend our gallant host in arms
And glory crown the brave whom honour warms."

19

Melverley Church.

Sandhurst Church.

Upton Church.

Slimbridge Church.

7. Royal Occasions.

The importance of Gloucester, Worcester and Shrewsbury owes not a little to the favour accorded them by the English kings. Ethelred II was crowned at Gloucester, and Edward the Confessor established the custom of holding councils there. William the Conqueror institutionalised "the wearing of the crown" every Christmas, and it was on such an occasion in 1085 that the council agreed to embark on the great survey of England, "how it was peopled and with what sort of men." Such meetings were splendid occasions from which Gloucester undoubtedly benefited.

Stephen and Henry II visited Worcester, and John was buried there. Owing to the loss of the crown jewels, his successor, the nine year old Henry III, was crowned at Gloucester with a golden circlet given by his mother. Edward I visited Worcester to pray at St Wulstan's shrine on eight occasions, and was present at the marriage there between Llewelyn and Eleanor de Montfort in 1278. He kept Christmas here in 1281 when "there was such a frost and snow, as no man living could remember the like." Edward II was buried at Gloucester, and a statue of Edward III adorns the tower of the Abbey Church in Shrewsbury. Henry IV used that town as his headquarters before the defeat of Hotspur in 1403, and the burial of Prince Arthur at Worcester was one of the last great mediaeval spectacles.

Thereafter the monarchy became firmly based on Westminster and, except for the coming and going of the Stuarts during the Civil War, royal visits became less frequent. But the authority of the crown became more widely proclaimed when Royal Arms were installed in every church in the land after the Reformation. Instituted by Henry VIII to symbolise his position as head of the Church of England, they were removed by Mary Tudor, replaced by Elizabeth I, destroyed under the Commonwealth, and reintroduced at the Restoration. Few have survived, but those of Elizabeth I may be seen at Ashleworth; of the Stuarts at Welshpool, St Nicholas, Gloucester, and Worcester Cathedral; of William and Mary at Lydney, and of Queen Anne at Tewkesbury. Over a dozen remain to proclaim the allegiance of the church to the house of Hanover.

Royal Arms of Queen Anne, Tewkesbury.

21

Boating at Upton.

8. Education and Entertainment.

Just as the river contributed to the prosperity of those living along its banks, so, it can be argued, did it provide a higher standard of cultural life than could be found in places isolated by bad roads for much of the year. The Severn, linking four county towns, two of the Three Choirs cities, a wide range of schools and libraries, and with plentiful entertainment arising from the social season which accompanied the assizes, was well ahead of the rest of provincial Britain. As John Wesley pointed out, communities which were not on a canal or river were "buried alive . . . (and) bred up for no other use than to feed themselves."

The grammar schools were, naturally, the foundation stones on which the cultural pyramid arose. Six were founded in the sixteenth century: Shrewsbury, Bewdley, Hanley Castle, St Mary de Crypt, and the King's schools at Worcester and Gloucester; and three in the seventeenth, Wroxeter, Bridgnorth and Tewkesbury. Most of them had similar aims to those of King's, Worcester, founded with confiscated monastic funds, "in order that in our Church, piety and good letters may ever bud, grow, blossom and in due season bear fruit to the Glory of God and the benefit and adornment of the Commonwealth."

There were also innumerable church charities supporting schools for the less privileged. The curate of Cressage was teaching the village children in 1576, but usually it was a woman, like the dame at Chaceley, teaching reading, knitting and church-going. Occasionally a village appointed a schoolmaster; Welshpool could only afford "a petty schoolmaster" whereas Westbury, in 1771, even provided theirs with a suit of clothes. The outfit, which cost over £3, included a pair of knee garters and "two dozen blue coat Death's Head buttons." In the nineteenth century the charity schools gave way to the National Schools, Gloucester's for instance, being opened by the Duke of Wellington in the year after Waterloo. By the end of that century, in contrast to today, there were few villages without a well established, purpose-built, school.

Public entertainment was centred on the four county towns, and especially Shrewsbury, Defoe's "town of mirth and gallantry." In about 1715, Gloucester and Worcester had combined with Hereford to produce a musical festival which was to become the most long-lasting of all. But long before that first concert, Worcester had shown that it had all the musical qualifications. The Duke of Beaufort, as Lord President of the Council of the Marches, visited the town in 1684 and was escorted to the Cathedral by the Dean. Then, according to his amanuensis, Thomas Dineley, "After Divine Service, His Grace was attended in great Order with Drums, Trumpetts, ye City Waites, Haut-bois, Flutes, other Wind Musick, together with Harps, Welsh and Irish Viols, Violins, and other stringed instruments to the Town Hall."

Not everyone enjoyed the Three Choirs concerts. Madame d'Arblay found them "very long and tedious" when attending George III at Worcester in 1788. She complained that the programme included a sermon and that she had "to stand perpendicular the whole time." There were even greater problems for lesser mortals, owing to overcrowding. The Reverend F. E. Witts gave a stirring description of the scene in Gloucester Cathedral in 1826, while the audience waited for the opening bars of Handel's overture "Esther": "An occasional scream or groan indicated distress or fainting. Some were carried out, some struggled into the outer choir, the most persevering stood their ground."

Cobbett, who had unwittingly arrived in Gloucester during the same festival, and found that to obtain a bed he would have to pay very high and bow very low, did not hide his feelings: "For what should there be here but one of those scandalous and beastly fruits of the system called a Music Meeting . . . They are amongst the profligate pranks which idleness plays when fed by the sweat of starving people. From this scene of prostitution and pocket-picking I moved off with all convenient speed, but not before the ostler made me pay 9d. for merely letting my horse stand for about ten minutes."

In spite of criticism, the festival has flourished. Fine choirs have been trained, great organs have been installed, composers like Elgar, who first played the violin at one of their concerts in 1878, have become its advocates; and the three cities have had the chance to listen to more great music than any other part of the provinces. It is indeed appropriate that the roof of the choir in Gloucester Cathedral should be adorned with angels playing mediaeval musical instruments.

Thomas Tomkins, who was at Worcester from 1596 for fifty years, was probably, with Elgar, the Severn's most distinguished local musician, and the Milton organ at Tewkesbury its most beautiful instrument. But there were amateurs as well, ranging from the beautiful and distinguished Mary Russell at Powick to the three choirmen whose death is lamented at Forden:

"Beneath this tree lies singers three
One tenor and two basses
Now they are gone, its ten to one
If three such take their places."

There was also the occasional individualist like Stephen Jeffries, the Gloucester Cathedral organist, who launched into "Lillibulero" as a voluntary at the end of the service celebrating the accession of William of Orange. It caused an uproar, "insomuch that the young gentlewomen invited one another to dance; the strangers cryed that it were better that the Organs were pulled downe than that they should be so used; and all sorts declared that the Dean and Chapter could never remove the scandall, if they did not immediately turne away so insolent and prophane a person out of the church." Jeffries, however, remained in office for another twenty-four years.

Musicians often travelled by river, as did the groups of strolling players who, with their collapsible booths and simple props, brought entertainment to its banks over many seasons. Local talent was used when available, as can be seen from a curious advertisement by the manager of Holloway's Portable Theatre at Newtown in 1876, asking for, "Gent for Heavies, Juvenile Gent and Low Comedian (to sing between the pieces) . . . A couple of Good Niggers. Send lowest terms."

Tomb of Mary Russell, Powick, by Thomas Scheemakers (1786).

The smaller travelling companies, offering long seasons, often performed at inns like *The Bear* at Welshpool or *The Red Lion* at Newtown. But they were at the mercy of the weather, a fickle public, Nonconformist opposition, and the village constable. Only the larger towns could expect visits from the London companies or leading players like Mrs Siddons and Master Betty, a Shrewsbury boy who played Hamlet at the age of sixteen in the Theatre Royal, Gloucester. Grimaldi also played in that theatre, being entertained by the notoriously aggressive Colonel Berkeley, who prided himself as an actor, and kept in his room a very appropriate picture of himself as Brutus slaying Caesar.

The more physical side of entertainment is depicted on misericords in many churches; jousting at Worcester, hawking at Ripple, and football at Gloucester. This last carving is almost contemporary with a visit to the town by the English Parliament in 1378. The monks, who had to hand over their quarters to the politicians and camp out in the orchard in mid-winter, complained bitterly that the abbey was treated more like a fairground than a religious house, "the grass in the cloister so trampled by wrestling and football playing that not a blade of grass was to be seen on it."

Bull-baiting, bear-baiting and cock fighting have flourished, especially amongst the Coalbrookdale miners. Wrestling took place in the quarry at Shrewsbury, and farm workers fought with colliers for possession of the top of the Wrekin at the May Day Wakes. One of the greatest prize fights took place at Worcester in 1842, when forty thousand people watched Langan and Springer fight eighty-four rounds for the championship of England, without interruption except when the grandstand collapsed. In a more genteel world, two great families, the Fosters and the Graces, established Worcestershire and Gloucestershire as first-class cricket counties, while Shrewsbury School has developed into one of the major forces in English rowing.

One man who saw the desirability of channelling some of this activity into more carefully controlled competition was Dr William Penny Brookes of Much Wenlock. He can well claim to have introduced the Olympics into the Severn valley long before the first International games were held in 1896. Passionately interested in physical education, he founded the Wenlock Olympian Society in 1850. He interested the King of Greece, who gave a silver cup for the pentathlon in the games held at Shrewsbury in 1877, and in 1896 was trying to organise the first Olympiad in Athens. He died a few months before it was held, so most of the credit has gone to his friend, Baron de Coubertin.

Back on the Severn, the activity which has, perhaps, had the widest appeal has been bell-ringing. Fynes Morison in 1617 thought England unique in its bells, "which men commonly ring out in musical tunes for recreation, which I never observed to be done in any other country." Tewkesbury has a chapel dedicated to St Dunstan, the patron saint of bell-ringers, and there are few churches on the river without their belfry rules. A popular rhyme, often copied, was in St Mary's, Bridgnorth:

"If that to Ring you do come here, You must ring well with
hand and ear, and if a bell you overthrow, four pence to
pay before you go, and if you ring with spur or hat, six
pence is due to pay for that, and if you here do swear or
curse, twelve pence is due, pull out your purse. Pay the
Sexton what's his fee, for he that swears shall not go free."

◀ Misericord showing Jousting, Worcester Cathedral.
W. A. Call

Misericord showing Football, Gloucester Cathedral.
W. A. Call

Bells, the oldest surviving musical instruments in most villages, travelled by water, and a large proportion of them came from the Rudhalls of Gloucester. Four generations of that family, from 1684 until 1828, cast some 4,520 bells, including the oldest in America. They were in a long local tradition which went back to Hugh the Bellfounder in the thirteenth century, John of Gloucester in the fourteenth, and William Henshawe, who was sheriff and five times mayor, at the beginning of the sixteenth.

Gloucester Cathedral has the only remaining mediaeval bourdon, Great Peter, inscribed *"Me fecit fieri conventus nomine Petri"*, (the abbey had me made in the name of Peter) with the arms of the abbey as stops in the lettering. It weighs 59 cwts and is reckoned to be the heaviest cast iron object of that period to survive. Gloucester also has a series of chimes going back to the sixteenth century. They include two tunes reputed to date from the tenth century, along with others written by their organists, or musicians associated with the festival.

The Minsterworth bells, which melted when the spire caught fire, were recast in 1903 with money from a lady who had in mind "the improvement and innocent occupation of the young men and lads of the parish by giving some portion of their evenings to the practice of ringing." This belief, that bell-ringing was a good thing because it kept young men off the streets, has never had much plausibility, as can be seen by consulting any set of belfry rules. Rule number 4 at Ashleworth, for example, makes clear what any young lad seeking improvement might come up against: "Drinking, Smoking, Loud Boisterous Talking or Jesting, and above all, Disputing are most unseemly . . . and are strictly forbidden in the belfry." But the country-wide custom of paying the ringers in ale made all such edicts difficult to enforce.

And outside the belfry, drink was often the labourer's most available pleasure. Doctor Johnson had acknowledged that "there is nothing which has yet been contrived by man by which so much happiness is produced as by a good tavern or inn," and in the countryside the ale-house was the one public building where all men could find relaxation, warmth, companionship, and once they had been established, the security of the Friendly Societies.

Not everyone agreed with Doctor Johnson, and Marshall deplored the practice of supplementing low agricultural wages with many gallons of cheap perry and cider, "an intolerable nuisance to husbandry" which encouraged idleness and vice. The trouble in Montgomeryshire was not cider or perry, but what Wyndham called, "a heavy glutinous ale." He found that where this was available "women generally survive the men, who too frequently fall an early sacrifice to intemperance." He admitted that there was, however, the compensation that visitors to the upper Severn were "rarely disappointed in finding a widow."

Belfry Rules, Forthampton.

Drunkenness, which seems to have been accepted in the rural communities, was more strictly treated in the factories around Ironbridge. William Reynolds' works had a table of fines which included two shillings and sixpence for bringing in a bottle, one shilling (5p.) for drinking it, and another shilling for getting drunk. The problem was not confined to working people, Lord Leighton of Loton remembering a party at which twelve gentlemen consumed thirty-three bottles of claret along with champagne and other wines at one sitting.* Nor was it, of course, confined to the Severn, although George Fox, who had an eye for such things, considered that he had never in all his life met with such drunkenness as he encountered when travelling from Tewkesbury to Worcester during an election campaign.

Marshall, trying to assess how much drink a Gloucestershire stomach could hold, was told of a labourer wagering that he could drink twenty pints straight, and finding that the twentieth overflowed from his mouth. From this he concluded that the capacity of the average man was two gallons and three pints.

*Three managed to drag themselves into the drawing room, the rest had to be carried up to bed.

9. The Antiquaries.

The Severn has been lucky in its topographical writers and its antiquaries. Leland, Camden, Defoe and Cobbett all visited the river, while the surveys published in the late eighteenth century for the Board of Agriculture provide more detailed information. William Marshall's *Rural Economy of Gloucester-shire* forestalled them by appearing in 1789. He was a farmer's son and claimed to be able to trace his blood "through the veins of agriculturalists for four hundred years." He submitted his first manuscript to Doctor Johnson who disapproved of his opinion that harvesting was permissible on Sunday. So he deleted the passage and published the book as "what Dr. Johnson approved, or let me put it in the most cautious terms, that of which Dr. Johnson did not disapprove."

Although fairly guarded about his own work he was cavalier in his denunciation of others in his field. He had an opportunity to do this when, in 1809, he produced a *Review and Abstract of the Reports to the Board of Agriculture.* The original report on Shropshire had been written in 1794 by J. Bishton, an experienced farmer, and Marshall had to agree that such a man could hardly write "without furnishing some portion of valuable information." The second report on that county was written by Joseph Plymley, Archdeacon of Salop, who admitted to being no practical farmer. Marshall thought this obvious, but agreed that the report revealed the archdeacon's benevolent disposition. And indeed, on the humane slaughtering of animals, and the plight of the agricultural labourer, he was ahead of his time.

The report on Worcestershire was written by W. T. Pomeroy who came from Devon to a county in which, as Marshall quickly observed, "he was pretty evidently a total stranger." The report, based on answers to queries, had little claim to originality. Marshall was on easier ground with the two reports on his own county, as both appeared "when the harvest had already been reaped." So George Turner, who wrote in 1794, was dismissed as a gleaner, and Thomas Rudge, in 1807, as the gatherer of the after-harvest, although as a non-farmer his qualifications even for that menial task were very incomplete.

There were also those who were not concerned wholly with agriculture. Some were clergymen like Robert Eyton, the rector of Ryton, who spent twenty-two years over his *Antiquities of Shropshire,* which was eventually published in forty-eight parts, comprising twelve octavo volumes. And there was Treadway Russell Nash, rector of Leigh, who drove to church in a carriage-and-four, "with servants afore him and servants ahind him," was an active magistrate, and published a fine edition of Hudibras. He spent the rest of his time compiling his collections for *The History of Worcestershire* which he published between 1781 and 1799. He was able to complete this great project, so he maintained, by living within his means, and eschewing "elections, gaming, horse racing, fox-hunting and other pleasures as are too frequently the ruin of county gentlemen."

Gloucestershire was well served by Ralph Bigland, Garter king-of-arms, whose *Historical, Monumental and Genealogical Collections Relative to the County of Gloucester* recorded innumerable churchyard memorials which have since disappeared. It was published by his son in 1791, after he had died. There were then already two county histories, the first having been published by Sir Robert Atkyns in 1712. It was a work which contained 73 copper plates by Kipp and has a disarming introduction, excusing it as the work of "a Lay Hand, whose true and hearty Love for his County excited him to this Performance." And it ends with the words, "May the great God who is the Author of Peace and the Lover of Concord evermore bless and preserve this County in all Peace and Happiness." He was followed by Samuel Rudder, a Cirencester printer, who used Atkyns' work to complete *A New History of Gloucestershire,* published in 1779, and considered by Horace Walpole, "the most sensible history of a county we have had yet."

There were many others: John Noake with his *Guide to Worcestershire* in 1868, Dean Cranage, whose *Shropshire Churches* in 1901 showed him to be, probably, the most knowledgeable churchman in the field of architecture who has ever lived, John Randall's *Severn Valley* in 1862, and Thomas Habington's *Survey of Worcestershire,* begun in the reign of Elizabeth I and not published until 1895.

Habington was, in many ways, the most interesting of them all. He was involved with his brother in the Babington Conspiracy and, as a result, his brother was executed and he himself spent six years in the Tower. He was released in 1592 and settled at Hindlip where he became expert in the construction of priests' hiding places. He was involved in the Gunpowder Plot when Henry Garnett, the Jesuit, was caught at Hindlip, but thanks, it is said, to the intervention of Lord Mounteagle, Habington was allowed to return to Worcestershire on condition that he never again left the county. Few men have made better use of such a restriction.

He lived to be eighty-six and spent the last fifty years of his life travelling round the county, copying epitaphs, recording family histories, examining churches and houses, and setting it all down in rich, elaborate prose. His great nail-studded trunk in the Tudor House Museum in Worcester seems typical of the rugged stamina of the man.

And he was one of the first to be aware of the pits into which all who follow his line of business will inevitably fall:

"In greatest antiquities are most uncertainties,
and when we have to saile by the card of
recordes and knowne evidences, wee are in
continuall danger to suffer shipwreck on the
rocks of ignorance."

CHAPTER ONE

Plynlimon to Llandrinio

FEW people would describe Plynlimon as an easy mountain to explore. Apart from the five peaks which give it a name, it is the source of three rivers, the Rheidol, the Wye and the Severn, as well as many smaller streams which are often indistinguishable from their more famous neighbours. The Reverend G. J. Freeman, after plodding, soaked to the knees, to the summit in 1826, described it as nothing but "a long and continuous bed of boggy vegetable earth." This was a description with which most early travellers agreed, and provides some excuse for Gough's map, in the late fourteenth century, showing the Severn rising in two widely separated lakes.

Five hundred years later, George Borrow was shown by his guide three possible sources, and was eventually persuaded to drink from what he was told was the real one; which he thought rather a shabby beginning for such a noble river. Borrow had acquired a fairly satisfactory pilot, but *The Cambrian Traveller's Guide* of 1840 would commit itself only to the discouraging statement that, "At a hovel . . . on the N.E. side , a conductor may sometimes be had."

Not many travellers enjoyed the expedition, Malkin described it as the most dangerous mountain in Wales owing to the swamps "which hold out no warning," and Thomas Roscoe thought the view not worth the perils risked, "even when the atmosphere is clear, which is rarely the case." *Black's Guide* in 1861 was even more disheartening: "Few travellers who make the ascent deem themselves recompensed for the toil and hazard by the desolate and cheerless aspect." But, provided one accepts another visitor's fairly superfluous warning that "the voluptuary will find little to detain him in these regions," walking on Plynlimon in high summer or on a bright March day can be an exhilarating experience.

Whether it is worth deciding which of the many springs gives rise to the Severn is another matter. It is, perhaps, easier to accept the fact that its source exists and pick it up before it enters Hafren Forest, a gloomy, thickly planted expanse of conifers, relieved here and there by clearings in which the Forestry Commission has allowed drifts of Yellow Pimpernel, Musk, Cow Wheat, and Devil's Bit Scabious to lighten their darkness. Under its Welsh name, Hafren, the river comes swiftly down through the Forest, with a spectacular waterfall at

Hafren Torri Gwdff, above Llanidloes.

Hafren Torri Gwddf (Severn-break-neck); and, by the time it reaches Llanidloes, it has dropped nearly 1,500 feet in about twelve miles. In descending the next five hundred feet to sea level, it will have to travel over two hundred miles.

At Llanidloes the Severn is joined by the Dulas from the south and the Clyweddog from the north. The valley of the latter is now a huge reservoir, the great wall of the dam towering over the derelict Bryn-Tail lead mine at its foot. In the 1870s, the mines in this valley were producing nearly seven thousand tons of dressed lead ore annually; but the remains of the Bryn-Tail are now an industrial monument on the banks of what is left of a stream which was once described to Edward Lhwyd as "a pleasant River for good and sweet fish, taken with snales, and in season from February till August."

The Severn enters Llanidloes by the Short Bridge and leaves it by the Long Bridge. Both were rebuilt in the first half of the nineteenth century. Henry Skrine saw the old wooden Long Bridge in 1798 and found it "very antient and much out of repair." It was used by carriages only in time of flood, as at other times it was safer to ford the river. Even today, Llanidloes takes little notice of the Severn, except for a short but pleasant bankside walk. Instead, the town's regular cruciform shape is centred on the timber-framed Market Hall.

It was built around 1600, and is the only building of its type surviving in Wales. That this has happened is something of a miracle, as some visitors, and most vehicle users, have looked upon it with hostility. Thomas Harral who, in 1824, was purporting to be appraising picturesque beauty on the Severn, called it "an ugly old wooden pile, disgracing its situation." Thirty years later a former mayor offered £53:15: 8 to have it removed, a local paper agreeing that, since it had been photographed, its removal would be an improvement. Mercifully, the authorities have resisted the temptation, and it now acts as an admirable brake on traffic coming from all directions.

The Market Hall houses the local museum which, surprisingly these days, still looks like one, rather than a boutique. Indeed, Llanidloes is pleasantly short on trendiness, its wide market streets being punctuated by functional establishments like Plynlimon House with its Royal Arms, and Siop yr Oen with its hanging sheep. This animal proclaims, as does the town seal, the importance of its fleece in the economy of the community.

The *Trewythin Arms*, the National Westminster Bank, and the grille of the New Market, add variety to what is a practical rather than a fashionable town. It is a tough, friendly place, as John Wesley found when, in 1749, he preached from the block under the Market Hall, with "the wind so piercing that whenever it came in my face, it almost took away my voice. But the poor people (though all of them stood bareheaded) seemed not to know there was any wind at all."

The Long Bridge, Llanidloes.

Many early Methodists, including Howell Harris and Daniel Rowland, used Llanidloes as a centre for missionary activity, and Nonconformity is still well represented by three large chapels. The uncompromising facades of the United Reformed and the Baptist, built within two years of each other, stare in confrontation across Short Bridge Street, while that of the Calvinistic Methodists stands aloof. At the other end of the ecumenical spectrum, Llanidloes produced one of the noblest of the Catholic martyrs, Richard Gwyn, recently canonised. A devout Welsh-speaking schoolmaster, he was arrested in 1580, tortured in six different prisons, including Bewdley and Bridgnorth on the Severn, then hacked to death at Wrexham by a bungling executioner. He is Montgomeryshire's only Catholic saint.

35

The parish church is dedicated to St Idloes, equally Welsh, but not recognised by Rome. It is a large building, notable for its magnificent roof, each hammerbeam adorned with a winged angel. One of them has the date 1542, which appears to be the year when this great mass of timber was transported ten miles over the mountains from Abbey Cwmhir, after Henry VIII had closed that remote monastery. Equally beautiful, and from the same source, is the early thirteenth century arcade. The ingenuity and exertion that must have been put into transporting so much heavy material over such difficult country, is indeed remarkable.

The report on Welsh Education in 1847 found that in Llanidloes "the upper classes appeared to understand English." Seventy years later, A. G. Bradley found the town Welsh-speaking but bi-lingual, whereas Rhayader, only ten miles away on the Wye, was wholly English-speaking. Both languages can be found on the many splendid slate tombstones in Llanidloes churchyard.

The castle dates from the twelfth century and now lies buried under the *Mount Inn*. The town which grew up around it received its first market charter in 1280, and thirty years later could boast sixty-six burgesses. Although Leland found that in all Arwystli there was "no pretty town, or any market but Llanidloes," it has never been over-prosperous. This was something with which the commissioners, inquiring into the state of the boroughs in 1832, agreed when they came to examine the civic regalia. All they could find were "two small maces of lead or pewter . . . the humble symbols of a poor but ancient municipality. The first regalia of infant Rome," they continued, "could not have been more mean than these."

What prosperity there was depended on the manufacture of flannel, and *Lewis's Topographical Dictionary* listed 6 carding mills, 18 fulling mills, and 35,000 spindles continually in operation in the town and neighbourhood in the 1830s. Originally the work had been done at home by women and children. "For wherein," asked a seventeenth century enthusiast, "can a woman better skill than in spinning and carding, and what can a child better do than pick wool or spin yarn?" Visitors remarked on the continuous sound of the looms from the open doors, and the acres of finished flannel lying exposed on the hillsides.

But competition from lower down the river and from Lancashire led to a decline, and the ensuing discontent, combined with opposition to the vast new Union Workhouses, led firstly to a violent attack on a Poor Law commissioner, and then, for a few days in 1838, to a group of Chartists taking control of the town. When this occurred, the Government reacted ineptly by sending down three very ineffective London policemen, and the disturbance was eventually suppressed by the Montgomeryshire Yeomanry.

The lesson of Llanidloes was not lost on the Lord Lieutenant, Lord Clive, and when much more serious strikes and demonstrations broke out at Coalbrookdale three years later, he acted with sympathy and restraint. When the trouble in Llandidloes was over, the town returned to its original role as a market centre for an area which Henry Skrine described as displaying, "a degree of rustic elegance . . . not incompatible with the general air of poverty and simplicity."

Beyond the Long Bridge, the valley opens out into what Camden called "good corne ground and meadow, with very much plenty of wood." Away from the river the land rises to a country of sheep walks, and even lower down, much of the timber has gone. Pennant who was here in the 1770s was surprised to find heart of oak being split and cut into roof shingles, when good Welsh slate was readily available.

For most of its course through Wales the Severn meanders in a north-easterly direction, and about five miles beyond Llanidloes it reaches Llandinam, a pleasant village, off the main road, and dominated by the church of St Llonio Lawhir. It was the mother church of Llanidloes and the country around, but the present building is largely the work of G. E. Street in 1864. The strong tower remains, as do some mediaeval pew-ends and a carving of Adam and Eve in the side chapel, but the rest is strictly Victorian.

The busy main road separates the village from the river, which is crossed by the first iron bridge to be erected in the county. It was designed by the county surveyor, Thomas Penson, and is guarded at one end by the statue of David Davies, a nineteenth century industrialist who was taught at the village school and then prospered to become one of the leading figures in the development of the mines and railways of South Wales. His statue is appropriately situated, as one of his first commercial undertakings was to build the approach roads and abutments for Penson's bridge. His descendants were great benefactors of cultural life in Wales.

About a mile to the north the Severn is crossed by another bridge, this time a stone one leading to Caersws. Although it lies low on the river, it was strategically important, and is overlooked by Cefn Carnedd, a superb hill fort, one of many sites claimed for Caradoc's last stand against the Roman legions. A folk hero, whose national standing has never been questioned, he was honoured by another Severn man, Edward Elgar, in the cantata "Caractacus".

Caersws was an important Roman station, the meeting place of five roads. Their first fort, a large one, lay north-east of the village on a spur overlooking the river. The auxiliary fort lies under the village, close to where the Carno joins the Severn. When Pennant was here in 1773, he found the fields divided by intersecting lanes, "as it were to point the very places which had formed the ancient streets."

Thomas Penson's bridge at Llandinam.

Thomas Penson's bridge at Abermule.

Thomas Penson's bridge at Newtown.

Although Caersws once had all the trappings of a mediaeval borough founded by the princes of Powys, Leland called it "famous in name but in dede a pore thrwghe faire," and Edward Lhwyd was even more explicit; "Now it is only famous for its Good Ale and handsome landladies. And a sumptuous Annual Feast bestowed upon Bartholomew's Day by the Titular Mayor who is always a Gentleman . . . After the Old Mayor's Treat there is a new one elected by lots out of a hat who hath nothing to do till the year's end. Then he invites all the Aldermen to hunt a hare upon Gwynfynidd."

The village became briefly important in the 1870s, when the Van lead mines above Llanidloes were connected to it by rail. And it was in the same valley, up towards Trefeglwys, at about the same time, that a reservoir was proposed, half the size of Loch Katrine, to provide London with its water. The scheme came to nothing, and Caersws had to content itself with becoming a controversial railway junction. Moat Lane took its name from the splendid motte at Rhos Ddiarbed, probably built by Roger of Montgomery before 1086. Unfortunately for passengers alighting at the junction, the station was half a mile from the road, and luggage had to be carried or trundled along a narrow, muddy path before one was anywhere near Caersws.

About a mile up the Carno valley is the small church of Llanwnnog. The walls contain stones from the Roman buildings at Caersws, but its greatest treasure is its rood loft. It dates from the beginning of the sixteenth century and is one of the finest in the country. Outside in the churchyard is the grave of John Ceiriog Hughes, once the Caersws station master, and a fine Welsh poet.

From Caersws the river wanders hesitantly through open water meadows before being constricted again near Newtown. To the south, a drove road leads from the river-crossing towards the Kerry Hills, its route marked by the hamlet of Little London*, a frequent place-name on such tracks. To the north, Aberhafesp Church and Hall stand high above the flood plain. The seventeenth century Hall is brick, and the Church has been restored in bright Victorian stone. The latter has a fine roof, some good monuments, and a churchyard dominated by a large marble angel, guarding the belt, sword and helmet of an officer in the 8th Hussars.

The parish remained Welsh-speaking well into the nineteenth century, and the 1847 Education Report was surprised that "the farmers are markedly ignorant of English, although the English language has recently spread widely along the left bank of the Severn." The Black Well, a medicinal spring, was held to cure scrofulous diseases; and a custom, known to Kilvert, of parishioners listening at the church door on All Hallows Eve for the names of those who were going to die in the ensuing year, seems to have persisted here into this century.

---

*Little Londons were encampments for Welsh drovers where there was shelter and food on the drove roads to the London markets.

Newtown is what its name implies, and its most recent transformation, when it received the dubious distinction of being designated a development area, was not its first. Edward I granted Llanfair Cedewain a market charter in 1279, so it grew up on a normal grid pattern. By mid-fourteenth century Newtown was replacing the Welsh name and Iolo Goch, Glyn Dwr's court poet, had called it "a municipality regulated like Paradise." Leland was less enthusiastic, though he admitted that "it was meately well buldyd after the Welche fascion."

The river above Newtown.

As at Llanidloes, sheep provided the prosperity, and a visitor in 1810 commented on the lines of women standing along the street with their baskets of spun wool, and the incessant rattle of the spinning wheels from the doors of the houses. It was an industry that went through the usual three stages: in cottages to begin with; then in weaving shops until the factories were built. These included the Severn Valley Mills and the Royal Welsh Warehouse. The latter now houses Kwik Save, in spite of a spendid Royal Arms defending the doorway, and PRYCE-JONES in huge letters dominating the town from the roof.

The Warehouse was built by Sir Pryce Pryce-Jones, the founding father of the mail order business. His new method of selling was so successful that the local railways introduced special vans, known as Mr Pryce-Jones' Vans, to take his goods to London and elsewhere. The Montgomeryshire Canal had already provided fresh outlets for trade, and the town's increasing prosperity had been acclaimed by a local bard:

"To London great, in short by the Canal
Thy flannel goes as quick as one can tell
And thence from there the flannel's quickly hurled
To every part of Britain and its known World."

Optimism grew, and Newtown was foreseen as "the busy Leeds of Wales:"

"Where cattle grazed and meadows once were green
Fair streets are formed and crowds of people seen
Industrious mortals seeming well to thrive,
All useful bees in the commercial hive."

Unfortunately, other bees in larger hives were providing increasing competition, and in spite of the reputation of Welsh woollens, the local industry went into a decline. Its memorial is the Newtown Textile Museum, created out of six small cottages, The Flannel Exchange, now the local cinema, and the Royal Welsh Warehouse.

The Pryce family had its fair share of eccentrics. Sir John, who had three wives, is reputed to have preserved in his bedroom the first two to die. They are commemorated in St David's church, Dame Mary as "a lady whose incomparable beauty and fine Proportions was the true Index of her sweet disposition of Mind, which shone through all the Cloud of Infamy which had been cast upon her Character by Envious and Malicious Persons." This was originally in the old church which was abandoned in 1840 owing to flooding. Its roofless nave still contains a curious Wendy-house of a mausoleum to the Pryce family.

More impressive than the mausoleum, is the grave of Robert Owen, the reformer and Socialist, who was born and died here, but made his name elsewhere. There is a bust by Alfred Toft over Owen's words: "It is the one great and universal interest of the human race to be cordially united and to aid each other to the full extent of their capacities." Around the grave the Co-operative Union erected a beautiful Art Nouveau railing, decorated with the words "Each for All."

The new church, St David's, was built by Penson in 1847. He removed the screen from the old church, but it was later cut up and used in the sanctuary and for a parclose. It had been one of the finest and longest in the county. It is a large church, and the splendid internal colour scheme on pillars and roof give it an individuality that few other Victorian churches possess. There is a fine lectern, the brass eagle poised above four bemused lions. Penson also built the Long Bridge, some twenty-one years earlier. It replaced a wooden bridge which had surprisingly withstood the 1795 flood.

The old church and Robert Owen's grave, Newtown.

It is a very Victorian town still, the Queen being commemorated by the tall town clock, a pub, and a window in St David's which shows her offering her crown to Christ. She was an early customer of the mail order business which may have enhanced her popularity. The Victorian impression is coloured by the number of Nonconformist chapels: Welsh Congregational, English Congregational, Welsh Calvinistic Methodist, English Calvinistic Methodist, Wesleyan Methodist, and the imposing Zion Baptist Tabernacle. All, with the exception of the Wesleyan (1835), were built between 1865 and 1881.

The Quaker Meeting House on Milford Road is much older. It once stood in the middle of Dolgellau where it was owned by a certain Lewis Owen who was murdered in 1555. It came to the notice of Sir Pryce Pryce-Jones who decided to remove it and re-erect it in Newtown in 1885. He was under the impression that it had once been Owen Glyn Dwr's Parliament House, a misguided view, shared by the 1979 official guide.

Montgomeryshire had Quaker leanings, and though many Friends suffered imprisonment there were sympathisers in high places. The yearly meeting for Wales was held in the house of the mayor of Llanidloes in 1697, and Charles Lloyd of Dolobran employed many of them in his iron forge at Mathrafal. Even Lord Herbert of Chirbury viewed them with a more understanding eye than many magistrates.

The Long Bridge leads to the parish of Llanllwchaiarn which now comprises a good deal of Newtown. There are two churches, one built in brick in 1815, and the other by Aston Webb for the founder of the mail order business in 1890. The earlier church looks across the river to the eleventh century Gro Tump, a motte that stands much higher than the later castle mound in Newtown Park.

42

The valley here is overlooked by the Kerry hills, a pre-historic ridgeway between England and Wales. It was also the grazing ground of Kerry sheep, a breed distinguished by a white head, black nose and black kneecaps, and notable for their very soft white wool. They were bred by John Wilkes, an influential farmer, who managed to persuade the Cambrian Railways to build a branch line from Abermule up the valley to Glanmule, where it was linked to neighbouring farms by a network of narrow-gauge tramways. It was not the sort of enterprise to appeal to Doctor Beeching, nor to survive him.

At Abermule, the river and canal travel side by side. The village, now a vast caravan encampment, has little to offer except Brynderwen Bridge, which was built for Thomas Penson by the Brymbo Company near Wrexham. The span over the river rests on huge iron letters: "THIS SECOND IRON BRIDGE CONSTRUCTED IN THE COUNTY OF MONTGOMERY WAS ERECTED IN THE YEAR 1852." It was near Abermule that the Cambrian Railways' worst accident happened when, in 1921, the Newtown slow train met the Aberystwyth express head on, and seventeen people were killed.

On the Welsh side of the river, Dolforwyn Castle, built by Llywelyn ap Griffith in 1273, guarded the cantref of Cedewain which Henry III had granted to him. When Llywelyn decided to add a market to that castle there was a swift English commercial reaction, and Roger of Montgomery destroyed it in 1277. He replaced it with his own new borough at Llanfair Cedewain or Newtown. There is little of Dolforwyn left, but the site is a marvellous one, high above the river, with command of the approaches from all sides.

Dolforwyn means The Maiden's Meadow, and it is in the river below that tradition has placed Geoffrey of Monmouth's story of Sabrina. Locrine, King of Loegria, fell in love with Estrildis after he was already pledged to marry Gwendolen. So, after the wedding, he hid Estrildis in an underground chamber where she gave birth to a child of great beauty who was named Sabrina. He then expelled his wife and made Estrildis queen, but Gwendolen raised an army, defeated and killed him, and ordered Sabrina and her mother to be thrown into the river.

In Milton's version, Sabrina underwent "a quick, immortal change" and became the goddess of the river, and so an object of veneration. He went on to describe how the shepherds, in praise of her, "Throw sweet garlands wreathed into her stream/Of pansies, pinks and gaudy daffodils." According to Dyer's poem on the story, it became customary to strew flowers on the Severn in her honour at shearing time.

After Abermule the canal turns away towards Berriew, where it crosses the Rhiw tributary on an aqueduct of five arches. It is a notable village of half-timbered houses, with an opulent vicarage of 1616 and a large Victorian church. The dedication is to St Beuno, a seventh century Welsh saint, and the circular churchyard must have enclosed several earlier buildings. A brief, issued in 1794, described the church then as, "so greatly decayed in every part that the inhabitants cannot resort there . . . without endangering their lives." The present building has good Elizabethan effigies of Arthur Price, fully armed and supported by his two wives.

Montgomery is two miles from the Severn, but is a town of too much enchantment to be omitted. Like Monmouth, it has the advantage of being a county town from which the bureaucratic machinery has been removed. It has thus been spared the profusion of presumptuous building that the re-organisation of local government has inflicted on so many places. The comments of Thomas Roscoe could still apply: "The town has an air of peculiar neatness and gentility, not very usual in the Principality. It is chiefly inhabited by persons of middle rank or small fortune, some of whom have selected it by way of economy, and some for learned leisure; they have everything which reason and nature can supply, and a succession of lovely and luxuriant scenes around them to charm the sight." *Lewis's Topographical Dictionary*, more primly, described it as, "well adapted to render it the residence of genteel families."

Although the area was strategically important from early times, the first Norman castle, Hen Domen, was built near the ford by Roger, Earl of Shrewsbury. He was entrusted with the pacification of the central March, and named the castle after his Norman home, Montgomery. In the reign of Henry III the old castle was abandoned for the present almost impregnable site above the town, a borough was created, town walls built, and the burgesses granted freedom of toll throughout the kingdom.

When Leland was here he referred to the castle as lately re-edified, and by that time the influence of the Herberts had become dominant. It was rarely challenged, but when it was, as in the 1588 Parliamentary election, resistance was absolute. In that contest, between Edward Herbert and Arthur Price of Newtown, every trick and subterfuge was employed by the sheriff in order to get his Herbert father-in-law elected. It is hard nowadays, amongst such tranquillity, to picture those "light and desperate men," armed with "divers kinds of monstrous weapons," guarding the Town Hall and castle, while the sheriff and one of his relatives plotted in bed together how to miscount Price's almost certain majority.

The Herberts continued to use the castle as a residence, and Lord Edward in the next century added a new section, making it into "an elegant and noble pile, beautiful without and richly furnished within." It was captured by Parliament in the Civil War, and although its captor referred to it as "one of the goodliest and strongest places that ever I looked upon," it was demolished five years later, and Sir Thomas Herbert, in 1680, described it as a horrid heap of rubbish and stones.

Herbert influence is also strong in the parish church of St Nicholas, a building which was contemporary with Henry III's castle. The roofing is complicated, being of different periods and ranging from the fifteenth century at the west end of the nave to the nineteenth over the chancel. There is a fine Royal Arms of 1726, some damaged misericords, an elaborate screen, hatchments (armorial tablets) and, above all, the superb tomb of Sir Richard Herbert, erected by his wife (who lies beside him) in 1600. Their eight children, including George Herbert and Lord Herbert of Chirbury, stand guard behind them, and the funeral tabard, which would have been carried before the coffin, hangs on the nearby wall. He is dressed in black armour, and his wife, Magdalen, has a red hair net and a long flowered dress. She married again and was buried in London thirty years later. John Donne, who wrote a poem for her on "The Primrose, being at Mountgomery Castle," preached at her funeral.

Broad Street, Montgomery.

45

The churchyard on the south side has been raised by constant burying to a height of six feet above ground level. This is not so on the north side, and it would be of interest to know when the traditional fear of being buried on the north, the Devil's side, succumbed to the needs of health and sanitation. There are no particularly old tombs, but the Robber's Grave attracts the visitors. John Davies was executed in Montgomery in 1821. He was found guilty of highway robbery, but proclaimed his innocence on the scaffold, and prayed that grass would never grow on his grave to prove it. His death, amidst lowering clouds and a violent thunderstorm, was watched by large crowds, and his grave, probably just outside the old churchyard, became a place of pilgrimage. It is now overshadowed by a white rambler rose, planted in his memory by an army pensioner; and there is certainly not much grass. He is watched from the west side by William Davies, a local policeman, whose marble tomb is carved with his helmet, truncheon, belt and lamp; while yet another Davies is commemorated on the south side as "keeper of the Goal in this town." He was also called John, but died nine years before his namesake. Viscount Torrington, who liked wandering in churchyards, noted here the grave of a man called Whatsoever Warmort.

Broad Street, the original market place, lies between the church and the Town Hall, which was built by the Herberts in 1748. It was enlarged for the Assizes by Thomas Penson in the 1830s, at about the same time that he was building the County Gaol at the lower end of the town. Although many of the original timber-framed houses have been re-fronted, the mediaeval street plan has not been changed. When Defoe came here, he observed that the inhabitants still proudly referred to the City of Montgomery. That such pride survives is shown by the admirably informative but unobtrusive notices put up at strategic points by the Civic Society.

It has always been a town of manageable size, and has had few critics. Even Torrington was delighted with the prospects although, as usual, he berated the accommodation at *The Green Dragon*; "Here began a specimen of Welsh dirt; for my blankets stunk so intolerably that I was obliged to use a quarter of a pint of brandy to sweeten them." John Aubrey called Montgomery "a most romancy seat," and it is today one of the most charming, well preserved towns in the March of Wales.

The road from Montgomery to Berriew crosses the Severn at Caer Howel on another of Penson's iron bridges, made by the Brymbo Company in 1858. It replaced a wooden bridge which broke under the weight of two waggons. The river here is flowing due north and is joined by the Camlad, a tributary which, with the Rea, formed one of the principal routes from Wales into England. This added to the significance of the ford of Montgomery at Rhydwhiman, protected from Forden Gaer by the Romans and Hen Domen by the Normans.

Largely due to the convergence of so many tracks at the ford, Montgomery was an important assembly area for the Welsh cattle drovers. Here the herds were collected and, where necessary, shod before setting out for Bishop's Castle. Then, using the commons and open hillsides for grazing, they moved through Plowden, along the Portway on the crest of the Long Mynd, to Shrewsbury and the English markets.

Forden, the Roman Lavobrinta, was also on the road from Caersws to Viroconium (Wroxeter) where there was another Roman crossing of the river. Forden seems to have been a cavalry station, providing escorts from the lead mines, and was abandoned in about 380 A.D. The area is now dominated by the Bryn Hyfrid Hospital, a severely classical, late eighteenth century brick building. It was once the Forden House of Industry, built to provide work for the poor of eighty neighbouring parishes. Its seal was an open Bible over a beehive, with the words "Religion and Industry produce Happiness," but, like so many of these vast consortiums, it produced more misery and discontent than happiness, and its industry was never as profitable as had been hoped. It is extraordinary that, nearly two hundred years later, and with so many other examples to learn from, we have still not absorbed the lesson that huge amalgamations, whether governmental, industrial, regimental or civic, are rarely as effective as the smaller local units they replace.

The church at Forden is Victorian and rather florid, but it contains an elegant oval font, given to an earlier building by Richard Edmunds in 1794. He also gave, according to *Lewis's Topographical Dictionary,* a Royal Arms, "exquisitively carved in wood, coloured and gilt," but this, much battered, is now in the Powysland Museum. The churchyard has some good examples of calligraphy on the headstones, especially those carved on slate.

More impressive examples of Victorian architecture will be found downstream at Leighton. The church and its adjoining hall were built in the 1850s for a Liverpool businessman, John Naylor, by a Liverpool architect, W. H. Gee. The Hall is enormous, with a Home Farm incorporating every advanced agricultural appliance. The gardens abounded in cascades and sculpture, and were surrounded by woods where some of the finest stands of Sequoia sempervirens, the true Redwood, were planted.

The church, equally impressive, has a commanding spire, elaborate pulpit, squire's pew and hammerbeam roof. The whole complex gazes defiantly across the river at Powis Castle, as if to show that Liverpool could do as much in seven years as the Welsh princes and the Herberts in seven hundred.

Powis Castle, a mediaeval fortress, converted into a Catholic stronghold by the Herberts, was visited by Leland when he could still remark on there being two castles within one wall. One had collapsed, but Lord Powis' was "meatly good." Sir Edward Herbert began to convert that castle into a dwelling house in 1587, but the major changes came after the Civil War. The Long Gallery and the state bedrooms bear witness to the extravagance of wealthy men reacting against the austerities of the Commonwealth. The Duke of Beaufort, as Lord President of the Council of the Marches, slept in the state bedroom when on tour in 1684, and his private antiquary, Thomas Dineley, wrote an admiring account of "the furniture of Crimson Velvet fring'd with Gold and ye ballasters . . . also richly guilded and diversify'd."

Not everyone was so impressed. There was a fire in the 1720s, and Henry Herbert's wife's addiction to high play was blamed for the subsequent impoverishment of the estate. So Torrington had plenty to get indignant about. He was appalled by its ruinous condition, "which reflects disgrace upon the owner; and sadly foretells the downfall of that empire, whence have fled honour and hospitality." He disliked the pompous bedrooms, found horses grazing in the parterres, and fruit unpicked in gardens which he considered had been laid out with wretched taste. "The only money that of late years has been (mis)spent here was to fit up over the old offices, a long narrow ball room . . . in which was given an entertainment when his l'dship came of age."

Matters improved, and in 1832, when Princess Victoria visited it, she was greeted by salvos from guns captured when the British stormed Seringapatam in India in 1799. Today it is one of the most important possessions of the National Trust, housing amongst other treasures, a beautiful miniature of Lord Herbert of Chirbury by Isaac Oliver, and the sword of the Lord of the Marches which was carried before Prince Arthur at Ludlow.

Welshpool lies deferentially outside the Castle walls. It has recently acquired that fashionable adjunct which has so often given the kiss of death to a rural community, an industrial estate. Welshpool is still very much alive, but what it has gained in size it has lost in character. Its Welsh name was Y Trallwng, after the pool near the Castle. Edward Lhwyd was told that it was "a very proud town, and there is an old prophecy that the pool hard by will swallow it."

Much of the pride and the Welshness seem to have gone, though the borough arms still contains Llywelyn's badge, Llysiau Llywelyn, the Germander Speedwell. Defoe found it "a good fashionable place," with many English inhabitants, while *Lewis's Dictionary* thoughts that its brick houses, built with an unusual degree of regularity, its lack of Welsh speakers, and its cheerful and prepossessing appearance, gave it the character of an English town. So it is perhaps appropriate that William Morgan, the great translator of the Bible into Welsh, should have been vicar here in Elizabethan times.

As a town, Welshpool probably dates from the first half of the twelfth century, and it received its first charter in the middle of the thirteenth. As with so many other new towns in the March, the charter was based on the laws of Breteuil in Normandy, and the setting up of a market led to a prolonged dispute with Montgomery over its functions.

Torrington, angry about Powis, was mellowed by the meal he got at *The Castle Inn*, "a very decent house." For three shillings, he and his friends were given a six pound salmon, a leg of lamb, peas and a tart. There are still plenty of good pubs, as one would expect in a market town, but traces of Defoe's "good fashionable place" are rare.

The Town Hall, erected in the eighteenth century, "at the expense of a few gentlemen . . . to avoid increasing the county rate," has been superseded by a rather pretentious building of 1873. And many of the pleasanter buildings, like *The Prentice Traders, Andersons,* and *The Mermaid,* all from the seventeenth century, *The Royal Oak* from the eighteenth, and the railway station from the nineteenth, seem to have been outnumbered by supermarkets and tasteless shop fronts.

The parish church stands above the town on an outcrop of rock, with a large boulder outside the porch. A strange tradition maintains that the boulder came from Strata Marcella, was originally in the church, and was thrown out by Parliamentary soldiers during the Civil War.

Adam of Usk, who escaped from Glyn Dwr's camp when he realised that he had picked the losing side, had a brief, unhappy stay here. A fugitive, arriving by night, he described in terms full of self-pity, his dishonourable predicament: "There in the parish church of the same, not daring to pass outside . . . like a poor chaplain, only getting victuals for saying mass, shunned by thankless kin and those who were once my friends, I led a life sorry

◀ The Montgomeryshire Canal at Abermule.

enough — and how sorry God in his heart doth know." As soon as a pardon had been obtained in 1411, he was away to England "with trembling heart but with a cheerful countenance." It seems curious that such a short and frightened sojourn should warrant the church guide calling him vicar.

He came here after the town had been sacked by Glyn Dwr, and that disaster may account for this embattled church's haphazard alignment of tower, nave and chancel. It has undergone many transformations in its time, but probably the most important were the addition of the south nave in the thirteenth century, and the building of a new chancel in the fourteenth. The former was the traditional Welsh way of enlarging a church, and the latter the system usually favoured by the English. Since then it has undergone other changes; the Elizabethan gallery, for instance, being removed in the eighteenth century because "the very common sort of people . . . (under the pretense of psalm singing) . . . run up and down there; some of them spitting on people's heads below." Later, there were two Victorian restorations.

The church contains a fine array of military colours and trophies. This was appropriate to a town which was commended by the Duke of Beaufort in 1684 for its militia's tactical skill and its officers' "very noble equipage." There is a superb Stuart Royal Arms, fine chandeliers of 1776, and a sixteenth century Flemish triptych. As at Slimbridge, the parish owns a golden chalice, given in 1662 by a governor of Guinea as a thank offering for his safe return. Pennant thought it worth £168 two hundred years ago but, unlike Slimbridge, the temptation to sell it has been resisted. Details of the gifts of other church plate, a christening bowl and "an elegant Silver Flagon" are described on the Benefaction Boards, which are decorated with the Royal Arms of 1778.

Welshpool has been lucky in its volunteers. The Llanfair to Welshpool narrow-gauge railway has been reopened by local devotees, and is one of the last of these admirable lines to survive. Similarly the canal is being restored and cleared by other enthusiasts. Small relics of Welshpool's past have found their way into the Powysland Museum in Church Street. This is another of the Severn's unpretentious collections, formed and housed by a local society. It contains a fine array of hatchments, and a splendid model of a guillotine, with victim in position, made from mutton bones by one of the Napoleonic prisoners-of-war quartered at Forden.

The Severn, now very tortuous, is bridged at Buttington, the scene of a battle in 894 A.D. between Danes and a combined force of Mercians and Welshmen. Three pits containing human bones were uncovered by workmen when building the foundations of a new school in the nineteenth century. Some three hundred and fifty skulls, unhesitatingly ascribed to the Danes, were extracted and displayed in the church for phrenologists to examine.

Offa's Dyke, which here approaches the river, disappears at Buttington, and there is a gap of over five miles before it begins again near Llandrinio. A suggested explanation is that the river was deliberately left undefined, or took the place of the Dyke, so that the many converging tracks would have easy access to an important river crossing. Leland refers to a bridge here; the present one, with its iron parapet, replaced a wooden structure in 1872. Buttington church is whitewashed and has a pleasant timber porch, dated 1686. It has a fine roof and a font made out of a thirteenth century capital which is said to have come from Strata Marcella.

This abbey lay beside the Severn near Pool Quay, and was partially excavated in 1890. Nothing now remains, though the original buildings must have been considerable. It was founded by Owain Cyfeiliog with Cistercians from Whitland in 1170, and rapidly acquired extensive possessions. These included grazing rights as far away as Plynlimon, lead workings in the hills, a windmill near Guilsfield, and rich pastures on the river plain. The monks had access to unlimited charcoal in the forests and water power from their weir, and it may well be that the iron industry carried on here by the Earl of Powis had its origins in the workings of the monks. The founder became a monk and was buried in the abbey church.

Pool Quay is now little more than a name on the map, though it has an expensive Victorian church. It was the highest navigable point on the Severn, and as a result, it became a place of some importance, with warehouses, a flannel mill, and lead works. Leland wrote of this stretch of the river, "the soile is wooddy, the valley cornefull," but today the woods have given way to rough pasture.

The whole area is overlooked by the Breiddin, an incomparable view-point, and the site of a great hill fort whose origins appear to go back to the Bronze Age. Replicas of its round Iron Age huts are in the Avoncroft Museum of Building. It was probably abandoned during the Roman occupation but was reoccupied when they left.

The Breiddin is crowned by Admiral Rodney's pillar, nominally celebrating his defeat of the French in the West Indies in 1781. But he had little to do with the county, and it is alleged that the pillar was erected by local landowners in gratitude for the money they had made during the war, as a result of his preference for English, rather than foreign, Navy timber. It was originally crowned by a ball, but this was not replaced after it had been struck by lightning.

The Severn turns east below Llandrinio, a parish which bestrides Offa's Dyke. The narrow bridge, steeply arched as at Atcham to facilitate the passage of barges, was built in 1775. Pennant described it as a new, handsome structure; and it is certainly one of the most graceful on the upper Severn. The church of St Trinio lies in a huge churchyard, and is basically a mediaeval building with Jacobean furnishings.

51

Llandrinio is a fair sized village with a number of good houses. It faces Criggion across water meadows which were once considered the most fertile in the Principality. This hamlet is a sad sight, lying as it does, under a seemingly permanent blanket of dust from the quarries devouring the Breiddin. Equally incongruous are the enormous masts and pylons of the nearby Maritime Radio Station. So the little brick Georgian church has much to contend with. But with its box pews, and its eighteenth century pulpit, it remains, along with the nearby Criggion Hall, a civilised survival from a more gracious age, in what is not far short of a disaster area.

The Breiddin from Llandrinio.

CHAPTER TWO

Llandrinio to Bridgnorth

FROM Llandrinio the river winds eastward towards Melverley and the English border. The Shropshire boundary comes down the Vyrnwy, past Melverley church, along the Severn for a mile and a half, and then south to the Prince's Oak near Alberbury. The tree is enclosed by masonry and the agreeable brass plaque which originally hung from its branches is encased in glass. Part of the inscription reads: "Near this tree His Royal Highness, The Prince of Wales, was introduced into his Principality . . . on the ninth day of Sept., 1806." Randall was of the opinion that all George did about his Principality was to break a small twig from the tree, put it in his hat, and return to the fleshpots at Loton Hall.

The Vyrnwy, one of the Severn's most beautiful tributaries, rises in a vast reservoir, constructed in the 1880s to provide Liverpool with water. It comes down through the magical valley which contains Mathrafal, one of the ancient capitals of the princes of Powys, and Meifod, the holy place where they were buried. The water authorities, in a well-meaning attempt to identify with the valley's historic past, designed the Valve Tower on the reservoir to look like the castle of Chillon on Lake Geneva.

Before the nineteenth century weirs were built on the Severn, the Vyrnwy was a famous fishing river, but Randall in 1860 was bemoaning the fact that very few of the twenty species of fish, enumerated by Pennant a hundred years earlier, could still be found. In its lower reaches the river floods along the water meadows, but Melverley church, high on its embankment, like Noah's Ark on Ararat, appears to be immune.

Indeed, entering the church is very like going aboard an Elizabethan galleon. As at Vowchurch in Herefordshire, it is as if the village carpenters had been given unlimited timber and a free hand to convert a barn. The simple black and white belfry gives no indication of the woodwork inside. The homely pews, the sturdy gallery which may date from the Armada years, the screen which, according to Dean Cranage, bore an inscription stating that church and steeple were rebuilt in 1718, are all in keeping with the candelabra and the oil lamps (in spite of the electric light bulbs they hold).

The river near Melverley.

Across the ugly bridge is Alberbury, very much a border parish which, in the late sixteenth century, had to ask for a bilingual priest, as many of the parishioners spoke nothing but Welsh. Only a portion of the castle remains and it is dwarfed by the massive tower of the church, consecrated by Bishop Swinfield in 1290, although it had been in use for many years. It is a large building, which was granted to All Souls, Oxford in 1441, and its most notable features are the magnificent fifteenth century nave roof and the Loton Chapel. Much of the striking nineteenth century restoration stems from the co-operation between General Sir Baldwin Leighton and his brother-in-law, the Reverend John Parker. The general, who joined the army at the age of thirteen and died aged eighty-two, provided the money, and Mr Parker, who had restored Llanmerewig and rebuilt Llanyblodwell, was the architect. They concentrated on the Loton Chapel, decorating the pews with finials and cherubs, and adding carvings to the roof timbers. The work has an individuality which distinguishes it from the unimaginative chancel that All Souls was building at the same time.

The interior is rich in monuments and hatchments to the Leightons of Loton and the Lysters of Rowton. The latter are in the nave, the memorial to Sir Richard Lyster, who died in 1691, having come from St Chad's in Shrewsbury. It is accompanied by a similar monument to Richard Lyster who died in 1766 after serving in five consecutive parliaments. The long eulogy concludes with the words; "His House like his Heart was open to his friends." Family memorials in the Loton Chapel include the broken propeller of the plane of Captain Leighton, M.C., who died of wounds when commanding 23 Squadron of the Royal Flying Corps. Perhaps the most pleasing of the memorials is the window designed with Art Nouveau glass for Sir Baldwin Leighton by his daughter, a friend of Burne-Jones. Loton Park, the family home, is a brick house which, like the church, has suffered many transformations since the seventeenth century when it was built.

The parish was the birthplace of Thomas Parr, "the old old very old man" who was born at The Glyn, lived through ten reigns, and was buried in 1635, at the supposed age of one hundred and fifty-two. Taylor, the Water Poet, described his diet:

"His physick was good butter, which the soil
Of Salop yields, more sweet than candy oil;
And garlick he esteemed above the rate
Of Venice treacle or best mithridate.
He entertained no gout, no ache he felt;
The air was good and temperate where he dwelt."

He should have stayed in that temperate air. Unfortunately, the Earl of Arundel decided to exhibit him in London, and inevitably, the journey, the London climate, and city food proved too much for him and he died soon after arriving, his only reward, a grave in Westminster Abbey.

Down by the river lay Alberbury Priory, founded in the thirteenth century by Fulk FitzWarine III, a local outlaw and popular hero, roaming the woods with his brother and friends, whose exploits are recorded in a French romance written during the reign of Edward II: "Greatly had he sinned against God by the slaying of people and other misdeeds, and to acquit him of his sins, he founded a priory in honour of Our Lady, the Holy Mother of the Order of Grandmont, near Alberbury, in a wood on the River Severn, the which he called New Abbey, the Old Abbey which he had granted to the Augustinians proving a failure." Leland visited it when it was "long syns suppressed," and the remnants are now marked by two farms called Red and White Abbey.

Camden thought Shropshire "not inferior to any in fruitfulness and pleasure," and this stretch of the river winds tranquilly through rich and pleasant pastures. Shrawardine and Little Shrawardine stand on opposite banks, but there is no bridge, and the ferry mentioned by William Worcestre has gone. The ford here was the northern boundary of the diocese of Hereford in Bishop Swinfield's day, and the castle which guarded it was a place of some importance.

Leland alluded to the tragedy which occurred on the battlements here when the child Richard FitzAlan was dropped to his death, "by the negligence of his nurse out of her arms." Most of the castle was destroyed after the Civil War, but according to the parish registers, the Royalist garrison perpetrated a considerable amount of vandalism before the war was over: "The church and chancel were puld downe; the Outbuildings of the Castle, the parsonage house with all Edifices thereunto belonging, and the greatest, fairest and best part of the Town were burnt for the safetye, as it was pretended, of the said garison."

For five years, while they were rebuilding the church, the parishioners used the castle stables for worship. The present building has an attractive eighteenth century atmosphere, with much plain panelling in the chancel and gallery. Its tranquillity matches the river, although even this placid stretch has witnessed its tragedies, Richard Mason, an honest and deeply religious young man, having been drowned with three others in a storm in 1652.

Montford village was described by Randall as "a quiet little place, the picture of rural security." Mercifully it is some distance from Montford Bridge which is not memorable for either quiet or security. The church was rebuilt in 1737, the money being raised by Brief, i.e. Royal mandate authorising collections for a charitable cause. £619: 3:11¼ was contributed but as almost half went on expenses, only £325:18: 4½ was received by the parishioners.

Charles Darwin's parents are buried near the tower.

There has been a bridge here since the thirteenth century when it was maintained by a wide variety of tolls, including 4d. on every tun of wine or cask of honey, 1d. on every horseload of lead, 1d. for every Jew on horseback and ½d. for every Jew on foot. Rafts and floats carrying wood paid 1d. when passing through, and there were provisions for compensation to be claimed if they damaged the bridge. It was almost as important a crossing as the ford of Montgomery; and it could be dangerous, as Edward III found, when £100 which had been forwarded to him by the Chamberlain in North Wales, disappeared with the messenger, who was drowned here, "by the rising flood of water, and could not be found, so that he was devoured by beasts."

When Leland visited these parts he found "a fayre stone bridge . . . a-late renewyd." Telford built the present one between 1790 and 1792 as part of the Holyhead road. It is now a hell of traffic, and one has only to stand near it for a few minutes in summer to wonder what has become of Housman's Shropshire, "The country for easy livers, the quietest under the sun."

After being joined by the Perry, the Severn twists north to the eighteenth century brick church at Fitz. The chancel was added in 1905 by Aston Webb and the pleasantly light building contains a Georgian Royal Arms, a gallery on iron columns, some delightful oil lamps, good church plate, and a plaque to an eighteenth century Senior Wrangler.* Like Alberbury, Fitz has enjoyed the attention of a clerical craftsman, Waldegrave Brewster, who carved the pew ends.

*The candidate placed first in the Mathematical Tripos at Cambridge University.

Fitz is high above the river which turns round The Isle, past Leaton, to within a few hundred yards of where the circuit began. The Victorian church at Leaton is as surprisingly unpredictable in its architecture as is the course of the river flowing beyond it.

Before entering Shrewsbury under the Welsh Bridge, the Severn passes the almshouses and chapel at Berwick. Hotspur is supposed to have spent the night before the battle of Shrewsbury here. Tradition tells how on the morning of the battle, as he assembled his forces, he realised that he had left his sword behind. When he was told that it was at Berwick that he had spent the night, he replied, "I perceive my plough is drawing to its last furrow, for a wizard told me in Northumberland that I should perish at Berwick, which I vainly interpreted of that town in the North."

Another tradition has it that he traced his hand with a knife on a panel of wood. A wise woman then pronounced: "Whoso by chance shall lose this hand/Will lose both name and house and land." The Betton family had owned Berwick since the fourteenth century, and the prophecy is supposed to have come true when Richard Betton, who was childless, lost the panel, and had to sell everything.

All the early visitors to Shrewsbury remarked on the way in which the Severn surrounds it. Leland, approaching from the English side, described it as standing on a rocky hill of sad, red earth, "and Severne so girdethe in all the towne that saving a litle pece . . . it wer an isle." Camden found it, "not only strong by nature but well fortify'd by art," while Thomas Churchyard, a Shrewsbury man, praised the fertility of the riverside:

"Full from Welsh Bridge, along by meddowes greene,
The river runs most fayre and fine to view;
Such fruitful ground as this is seldom seene."

And indeed, the distinctive skyline, the parkland sweeping down to the unfenced river, and the Severn itself, still give the town the charm that Housman remembered when he wrote, "High the vanes of Shrewsbury gleam/Islanded in Severn stream."

The wealth which produced this noble prospect came from its central position, its navigable river, and its close commercial links with Wales. Its importance was established, as a town with five churches and its own Saxon mint, long before Roger of Montgomery began building his Norman castle and demolishing fifty-one houses in the process. Within the next two centuries, most of the churches were rebuilt in stone, a Benedictine abbey founded, the walls completed, friaries established, and a monopoly of the wool trade acquired, which made it into a Welsh metropolis.

Defoe found it "a beautiful, large, pleasant, populous and rich town, full of gentry and yet full of trade too . . . which enriches all the country round." He thought the inhabitants were mainly English, except on market days when one would think one was in Wales. Camden had found the town equally divided between the two races, and many people bilingual.

By the seventeenth century the Drapers' Company was dealing with almost all the cloth being produced by Welshmen, and a hundred years later Pennant commented on the great profit Shrewsbury derived from Montgomeryshire. At the Thursday market he noticed "700,000 yards of Welsh Webbs, a coarse woollen cloth, dressed by Shearmen, and sent to clothe American negroes and Dutch peasants." The shearmen, who had been incorporated by Edward VI, carried his effigy in honour at their feasts and processions.

It was a system in which the Welsh had most of the risk and labour, and the Shrewsbury merchants the power and the profit. And as Doctor Johnson found out, it had certain unpleasant side effects. Boswell described how the doctor was buttonholed by a learned gentleman who told how "Counsel upon the circuit at Shrewsbury were much bitten by fleas . . . He in a plenitude of phrase told us that large bales of woollen cloth were lodged in the town hall; that by reason of this, fleas nestled there in prodigious numbers; that the lodgings of the counsel were near to the town hall; and that those little animals moved from place to place with wonderful agility. Johnson sat in great impatience till the gentleman had finished his tedious narrative and then burst out (playfully however), 'It is a pity, Sir, that you have not seen a lion; for a flea has taken you such a time, that a lion must have served you a twelvemonth.' "

When Cobbett arrived on a Fair Day, in what he described as "one of the most interesting spots that man ever beheld," he found everything in decline, the Drapers' Hall abandoned, and Welsh merchants going elsewhere. The folklore of that abandonment blames the greed of the local merchants who devised a barrel, exactly a yard in circumference, on which to wind and measure the great strips of cloth, often as much as one hundred and twenty yards long. Welshmen, it was claimed, could not understand why cloth measured at home was so much shorter in Shrewsbury; so that when at last the light dawned, they abandoned the town for ever. Certainly, by 1813, the Shearmens' Hall was being used as a tea warehouse.

Henry Skrine tended to agree with Cobbett, admiring the setting but deploring "the interior of this place, woefully deficient in convenience and accommodation, the pavement execrable and the buildings for the most part indifferent." Torrington, in a bad temper because of the weather and his room at the *White Lion,* ("a noisy, dirty, cold hotel; but good port wine") was equally unenthusiastic. He found the streets slippery and uneven, Gwynne's new English Bridge too narrow and its balustrade and ornaments clumsy, the market house woefully ill-kept, and the town altogether "a melancholy unlighted place, devoid of every public exhibition."

The distaste which travellers felt for Shrewsbury is surprising. It was the county town, with the customary assizes and accompanying season of social events, races, balls, banquets and plays, for which the gentry and their families assembled. Defoe called it, in earlier days, "a town of mirth and gallantry," and Celia Fiennes, earlier still, had been impressed by the abundance of quality. Indeed, most of the visitors were more appreciative of the inhabitants than of the town itself.

Cobbett was delighted with their friendliness and, perhaps more important, by the surprising number who came to listen to him. John Wesley, too, who had suffered several noisy meetings on previous occasions, was pleasantly astonished when he opened the new preaching house: "I did not so much wonder at the largeness as the seriousness of the congregation. So still and deeply attentive a congregation I did not expect to see here. How apt are we to forget that important truth, that all things are possible with God."

Much of Shrewsbury's entertainment took place in the Quarry, still one of the town's great amenities. Prince Arthur attended the play there, the Elizabethan militia mustered there, a woman called Foxall was burnt there in 1647, and Boswell and Doctor Johnson strolled there.

The English Bridge, Shrewsbury.

The fine iron gates were presented to the corporation by The Shropshire Floral and Horticultural Society in 1881, and the Quarry is now best known for its gardens and the Shrewsbury Flower Show. When Celia Fiennes was here she found "nothing fine nor worth notice save the Abbey Gardens," their gravel walks lined with orange and lemon trees, a greenhouse "full of all sorts of Curiosityes," and the grass "kept exactly cut and roled for company to walk in." Every Wednesday, she noticed, "most of the Ladyes and Gentlemen walk there as in St James' Park."

She went on: "It's true that there are no fine houses but there are many old large houses that are convenient and stately." Some had been built by merchants like William Rowley, the friend of Richard Baxter, or by Robert Ireland, whose handsome timber-framed home still adorns the High Street. Randall found many of these fine houses empty when he was writing in 1860, "with ceilings, mouldings, panellings, fireplaces and carvings torn down, whilst their outer shells serve as storehouses for bark and timber."

The destruction did not end there, and much of Shrewsbury's admirable mixture of Georgian and earlier buildings has succumbed to the usually incongruous supermarket or nondescript store. Even the unique Victorian Market has been replaced to speed the flow of traffic. But much remains: the castle, high above the river and the grandiose railway station; Laura's Tower and Telford's other work in the castle grounds; the Music Hall and the Royal Salop Infirmary, both by Edward Haycock, a local man; the Old Market Hall; Sir Robert Smirke's dignified Shire Hall; and the compact mediaeval core of the town with its evocative street names: Mardol, Wyle Cop, Dogpole, Murivance, Grope Lane.

As yet unspoilt, is Shrewsbury's marvellous riverside, with its famous bridges. Leland described the Welsh Bridge as "the greatyste and fayrest . . . having 6 great arches of stone . . . and at one end of it a great gate to enter by into the towne and at the other end towards Wales a mighty stronge tower to prohibyt enemies to enter into the bridge." It had been the scene of a bizarre incident when Henry, Earl of Richmond, tried to gain admittance on his way to Bosworth Field. Thomas Mytton, the chief bailiff, barred the gate and announced that he would be "slain to the ground and so run over," before he would let him enter. Henry retired and returned on the following morning to assure the bailiff that he meant no harm. So after deliberation with his fellow councillors, Thomas Mytton made good half his vow by opening the gate, lying down on the bridge, and letting Henry ride carefully over him. Another, less exciting version of the story in a ballad, "The Rose of England", confirms the bailiff's defiance but omits the charade on the bridge.

Pennant found that the gate had been demolished by the corporation, "to the regret of every person of taste," and the bridge soon followed, to be replaced by the existing structure in 1791. On the eastern side of the town was the English Bridge, which in Leland's time had four great arches and a drawbridge. Pennant thought it a "very ancient and incommodious narrow bridge, with the usual obstruction, a gateway." The Burghley map of 1575 shows two gates, one of which is in the middle, with houses on either side. It was replaced in 1769 by John Gwynne's present bridge.

There are also the churches, of which the grandest is St Mary's, on the site of its Anglo-Saxon predecessor. The fine chancel arch and thirteenth century arcades make the church and adjoining Drapers' Chapel high and spacious, and the whole building is lit by the most splendid glass, some in the Jesse window from the church of the Franciscans, much of the rest from Germany and the Low Countries.

The church contains an eighteenth century Royal Arms, a collecting box with the words "Pray remember the Brief," and some fine monuments. They range from the beautifully incised slab of Nicholas Stafford and his wife in her elaborate fifteenth century headdress, to the bust of Admiral Benbow, presiding over the battleship on which he died of wounds in 1702. The inscription lauds him as the toast of the British Navy and "the Nelson of his time," but John Evelyn had a different opinion of him. He leased his house to him and found him, "not a polite tenant." Moreover, Benbow sub-let it to Peter the Great, who made the house "right nasty" and destroyed Evelyn's prized holly hedge by riding through it in a wheelbarrow.

The parish church of the Corporation is St Chad's, originally another Saxon foundation, and hence dedicated to a Mercian bishop. The present building was erected after the old church, in 1788, "sank to the earth with so little noise that no person . . . nor even the watchmen were alarmed." Subsidence of old workings below was believed to have caused the trouble, and the building of a new church in four years was a remarkable achievement, in view of the difficulties that had to be overcome.

James Wyatt was entrusted with the task but proved so dilatory that George Steuart, the builder of Attingham, was called in. His choice of a site, on the town walls overlooking the Quarry, aroused opposition, as did his plans for a circular church, the committee only agreeing to the latter when they realised that new designs would increase the cost. In spite of petty squabbles over the width of the seats, and more serious arguments over whether there should be a spire or a cupola, along with quarrels over the competence of the surveyor, the building was opened in 1792.

The church is a succession of surprises, passing from the circular vestibule to the oval space containing the graceful gallery stairs, and then into the beautiful circular nave. There is a fine series of hatchments around the gallery walls, and the monuments of two of those concerned with the building; William Hazledene, the ironmaster who produced the railings, and John Simpson, the surveyor.

The vestibule has memorials to men of the 53rd Shropshire Regiment who died in the Indian Mutiny; and St Aidan's Chapel has been admirably converted into a shrine to the men of the King's Shropshire Light Infantry and the Herefordshire Regiment, who died in later conflicts.

There are many other churches in the town; St Alkmund's, with nearly as fine a spire as St Mary's; St Julian's, with its pinnacled tower; and Holy Cross in Abbey Foregate, under constant threat of flooding. The registers of this church are much concerned with the problem. In 1610, for instance, "Bricke to pave ye Churche after ye great inundation;" and 1614, eighteen pence "for stoppinge of water of Seaverne out of the churche, being then a mighty great flood." The *Shrewsbury Chronicle*, describing the damage after the great flood of 1795, found the gravestones all out of place, "which make a most awful and striking appearance and puts us in mind of the general Resurrection when it is said the graves shall give up their dead." On the parish War Memorial is the name of the poet Wilfred Owen M.C.

The seventeenth century buildings of Shrewsbury School are now the Library and Museum. The figures of Polymathes and Philomathes guard an inscription in Greek to the effect that "If you love learning you will be learned." Camden, once headmaster of Westminster, called it "the best filled school in all England," and considered the library not inferior to that of many university colleges. The Duke of Beaufort visited it in 1684 and was presented by the Corporation with twenty chargers of sweetmeats and two hundred and forty bottles of wine.

Although Defoe admired the school library, he was not shown any manuscripts or rarities. Indeed, when Butler became headmaster he found the library being used as a hairdressing saloon, and had to circularise all booksellers in the county asking for any school books to be returned. Amongst the first pupils were Fulke Greville and Sir Philip Sidney who entered the school in 1564. It has now moved across the river into buildings which began as the Orphan House for children from Captain Coram's Foundling Hospital, and then became a workhouse. When Celia Fiennes was here she was more interested in "a very good Schoole for young Gentlewomen for learning work and behaviour and musick."

Shrewsbury has honoured several of its notables with statues. Sabrina, Sidney, John Howard, Lord Hill and Lord Clive, who was mayor in 1762, are commemorated; but Darwin, whose father was a greatly loved doctor, remained unrecognised for some years. Randall, writing in 1882, deplored the fact, and accused the civic leaders of doing nothing but wait, "trembling as though the firm basis of their faith were shaking beneath them as each new truth was promulgated." His effigy was eventually placed in front of the Library fifteen years after his death, a much speedier recognition than that granted to Sir Philip Sidney who had to wait nearly three hundred and forty years for his statue.

After passing under the English Bridge, the Severn turns north to the aptly named Ditherington where it again changes course and wanders unsteadily towards Uffington. Ditherington contains the first cast-iron-framed building ever erected. It was made as a flax-spinning mill at Coalbrookdale in 1796 and was almost as great an innovation as the Iron Bridge.

Uffington, a village with a Victorian church and a pleasing water front, is shut in between the river and the old canal. Behind it lies Haughmond Abbey, near which the battle of Shrewsbury was fought in 1403. Henry IV and his army forded the Severn at Uffington and waited near the abbey for the Percies to arrive from Berwick. There were great casualties on both sides, but Hotspur's death decided the outcome. The body of "the flower and glory of Christian knighthood" was dug up and displayed in Shrewsbury, impaled on a spear set in a millstone. It was then beheaded and quartered and the parts distributed to York, London, Newcastle, Chester and Bristol. Three months later the King ordered the parts to be returned to Hotspur's widow, and three years later the memorial chapel was founded at Battlefield, with chaplains to pray for the souls of the King and of those who died in the battle. It became the parish church after the Reformation.

The river at Uffington.

The river continues southward, past the site of a weir that once belonged to the monks at Haughmond, and past Longner Hall to Atcham. The Hall was built by John Nash in 1803 on the site of an older house. A stained glass window on the staircase commemorates Edward Burton, a devout Protestant who, having endured the reign of Mary Tudor, is alleged to have died of joy when he heard the bells of Shrewsbury ringing for the accession of Elizabeth I. He was buried in the grounds.

Longner adjoins that other resplendent Nash house, Attingham. It was designed by George Steuart in 1782, in front of an earlier house, Tern Hall. Steuart planned it as a set of rooms for the male members of the family on one side of the entrance hall, with matching appartments for the womenfolk on the opposite side. Nash's contribution to the building was the conversion of the hall into a picture gallery, with an iron-framed ceiling which was cast at Coalbrookdale.

The grounds were first laid out by Thomas Leggett in about 1770. Torrington found them ugly and "flat with small circular plantations," but admired the bridge which Robert Mylne had built over the Tern in 1774. Humphrey Repton was commissioned to lay out the grounds afresh in 1797 and his Red Book is still in the house. He widened the Tern, cleared its banks, demolished the remaining mills and forges, and moved the cows away from the house, "for cows are peculiarly useful in showing the extent and distance of a plain surface." But his idea of putting a spire on Wroxeter church tower to improve the prospect had to be abandoned when he found that Lord Berwick did not own it. Attingham now belongs to The National Trust.

Attingham House.

Atcham Bridge.

Before reaching Atcham, the Severn passes under John Gwynne's elegant bridge. There were earlier bridges here, the first probably built by an abbot of Lilleshall to replace a thirteenth century ferry. Leland found "a fayre stone longe bridge" and Gwynne's followed in 1769. He was a founder member of The Royal Academy, a friend of Doctor Johnson, and the builder of Magdalen Bridge, Oxford.

Atcham lay on the Holyhead Road and once had eighteen coaches a day passing through. It must then have been a haven of peace in comparison with the situation today, as high speed traffic, encouraged by the building of a wider bridge, slices through this delightful village. When petrol runs outs, it may return to the tranquillity it deserves, as it has retained most of the ingredients of a civilised community, a majestic pub, red brick village houses, the noble gates of Attingham, and a fine church overlooking the river.

It is dedicated to St Eata, "the gentlest and simplest of men;" a curious dedication as he was a northerner with few obvious connections with these parts. The tower has Roman stones in its base and once boasted a spire. This was struck by lightning in 1879 when the choirboys were in full song. Several were injured, and the Shrewsbury Museum has a grisly collection of their boots, shrivelled, curled and mutilated, supposedly by the lightning passing through their feet.

65

The valley near Leighton.

The timber-framed porch is dated 1685 and the font, with the wardens' initials, ten years earlier. There is a chaste screen from near Bridgnorth, an elaborate vicar's stall, and a beautifully incised slab to Edward Burton and his wife from Longner. He was Groom of the Stool and Master of the Robes, and died in 1524. They lie together in flowing robes, long hands clasped in prayer, their children at their feet. Other Burtons are commemorated, including Henry who was vicar here for fifty years. His enormous monument seems out of keeping with the character it ascribes to him of being, "devout, serene and humble."

And humility hardly seems to have been the dominant characteristic of his wife. On a visit to Bacton in Herefordshire in search of her ancestors, she found a fine monument to Blanche Parry, not only one of the family, but also "chief gentlewoman of Queen Elizabeth's Privy Chamber." She seems to have had qualms about removing the monument, but none about extracting some good fifteenth century glass showing the family of Miles ap Harry, which she inserted in the east window at Atcham. She also had the Bacton monument copied on glass and placed it in a window in the north wall of the nave. The church has other good memorials; one, to Stephen Sayer of the King's Dragoon Guards, who died at Waterloo, chooses its words with circumspection:

"No further seek his merits to disclose,
Or draw his frailties from their dread abode."

The Tern, coming down through Attingham deer park, joins the Severn half way between Atcham and Wroxeter, the Roman Viroconium. Originally a military outpost of the Empire, and then the tribal capital of the Cornovii, it was linked with London by Watling Street, now ignominiously graded A 5. Telford, who claimed to have discovered the Roman baths, was commissioned by the lord of the manor to excavate Viroconium, "in order that men of learning might satisfy their curiosity." He was directed by local farmers who could trace the foundations of the buildings through the scorching of corn during dry weather.

Telford's was by no means the first excavation. As early as 1292 four men had been accused of digging for treasure by night, and according to Leland, Wroxeter provided the stones that gave rise to Shrewsbury in exactly the same way that the stones of Kenchester gave rise to Hereford. The Roman city covered an area of 180 acres, and the western defences seem to have suffered from the river. The crossing was below the island at Brompton Ford. Camden noticed that the foundations of a bridge were revealed here when a weir was being built, and this was confirmed by excavation in 1926.

Some of the stones of Viroconium certainly found their way to Wroxeter church, where the gate is flanked by two Roman pillars and the font seems to be the base of a column. There is also Saxon work in the north wall and an impressive Norman chancel. The furnishings include box pews, communion rails dated 1637, a thirteenth century chest, and four superb table-tombs.

The earliest (1555) commemorates Lord Chief Justice Bromley and his wife, "on whose Sowles God have mercy." Although he was one of Henry VIII's executors he was accused of being "a Papist at heart." He and his wife lie side by side, as does their daughter with her husband, Sir Richard Newport, on another tomb. The figures are alabaster, and the mourners around the Newport tomb are holding shields, like matadors with their capes. Not all in this family were papists at heart, and one who died in 1610 is recorded on his brass as having "lived and died hating and detesting the church of Rome as it now standeth."

The church has suffered from neglect. The Royal Arms, together with the altar piece, cost £18: 9: 0 in 1765. Today the rotting canvas droops from the frame and the roof seems to leak, as it must have done in 1709, when a man was paid 4d. "for carrying out ye snow 3 times." Richard Baxter went to school in the church, and for a short time taught here. There are two bells from the reign of Elizabeth I, one of them inscribed:

> "God save the Church Our Queene & Realme
> And send us Peace in Christ. Amen"

From Brompton Ford, the Severn runs southward and straight until it is joined by the Cound Brook opposite Eyton. An attractive octagonal summer house is all that is left of Sir Francis Newport's great mansion. Lord Herbert of Chirbury was born there, in the home of his maternal grandmother.

Tomb of Sir Richard Newport (1570), Wroxeter.

Cound church has a distinctive pinnacled tower and a number of opulent memorials to the Cresset family of Cound Hall, a Queen Anne house lying between the church and the river. The most important member of the family and the one with the most impressive memorial was Dr Edward Cresset (1755). He became Bishop of Llandaff, a fact symbolised by his mitre and crozier amongst more worldly trophies on the monument. John Cresset Pelham is also commemorated here. He was Member for Shrewsbury and played a large part in the repeal of the Salt Tax in 1825. One of his election posters warned the advocates of the tax to remember Lot's wife.

The church was heavily restored in the nineteenth century, but part of a painting over the chancel arch was spared, along with some mediaeval floor tiles. So were a Norman font, a Jacobean pulpit, a large thirteenth century chest, and a fine closing ring in the south door.

A ferro-concrete bridge has supplanted Telford's timber one at Cressage, a village once known as Cristesac, and hence one amongst many claimants to be the site of St Augustine's Oak. It is still remembered for its oaks, The Gospel Oak, The Curst Oak and The Lady Oak which, in Randall's time, consisted of a young tree growing from an acorn which had been dropped inside the hollow shell of a much older, dying tree.

The church was originally dedicated to St Samson of Dol, a sixth century Breton saint. It stood in a field nearer the river, and was so frequently flooded that Christ Church replaced it on safer ground in 1841. The gallery, like Fitz, stands on iron columns, and the pulpit has the curious inscription: "Hovmfry Dalle the eldar made this for James Dalle which I Pray God to bless unto his end Amen 1635."

◀ The remains of Viroconium, with the Wrekin in the background.

Cressage was a Saxon settlement with fishing rights in the river at Domesday. Later, Buildwas Abbey acquired loading facilities for barges here, as well as permission for the monks to dip their sheep. Randall enthused about the fishing on this stretch, where many of the finest Severn salmon had been caught. He advocated red worms, wasp grubs and, in autumn, new bread for roach and dace. The water was also notable for grayling, chub, perch and giant pike.

Eaton Constantine lies on the east side of the river, and the house where Richard Baxter lived as a child still honours him with his name. The whole area is overlooked by The Wrekin which, in Leland's time, "standeth as a Pharos, barren of wood." On the summit he admired the fine grass and a fair fountain; today it flaunts a television mast.

The church at Leighton, standing in the grounds of the Hall, with marvellous views over the valley, signals the approach of Coalbrookdale with its iron monuments, one in the floor of the nave dated 1696, and a more elaborate one in the churchyard from 1828. The church was built in brick in 1714 and the Hall about seventy years later. The earlier monuments to the Leighton family include a thirteenth century knight and a sixteenth century incised slab. There are also memorials in the nave to the Kynnersley family. The Royal Arms are of George I and the font is shaped like an urn. Leighton was the birthplace of Mary Webb, the novelist.

The valley closes in as the river approaches Buildwas, the parish church on one side and the great Cistercian abbey on the other. The church, which is almost contemporary with Leighton, has the date 1720 on a cast-iron plate in the porch, and a huge iron-topped tomb in the churchyard to John Wilkinson who died twenty years after his more famous namesake. The church is guarded by a curious iron gate, decorated with painted arum lilies.

The abbey was founded in 1135 and became Cistercian twelve years later. A great deal has survived and, although it has become separated from the river by the railway line, it remains a peaceful retreat from the crowds and traffic at Ironbridge. It was not always so. An abbot was murdered by one of his monks in 1342; eight years later his successor was abducted into Wales; and at the beginning of the fourteenth century it was devastated by Glyn Dwr. Even so, there were seven Cistercians here when the abbey was closed in 1535.

As at Tintern, where the abbey forges foreshadowed the later industrialisation of the lower Wye valley, so at Buildwas there was a monastic forge which was taken over by speculators at the Dissolution. Torrington deplored the destruction of many buildings shown on Buck's map, which had been made only fifty years before his visit. He considered it wicked that such places could be regarded as nuisances, and their stones and roofing employed in the repair of roads and pig-styes. This righteous indignation did not restrain him from prising some mosaics from the pavement for his own collection.

Ruins of Buildwas Abbey.

Leland described a stone bridge here, "else there is none between Atcham and Bridgnorth." It was swept away in the 1795 flood, and Telford was commissioned to replace it. It was his first iron bridge, and although the span was thirty feet greater than that of the Iron Bridge downstream it used two hundred fewer tons of metal. Unfortunately, this, too, was destroyed when the present commonplace structure was built in 1904.

Torrington approved of Buildwas, calling it sweetly situated. "All this vale," he wrote, "is a most sumptuous garden, so water'd, so wooded, and so studded with good houses." Here too was a row of poplars, The Twelve Apostles, reduced to eleven when Judas was conveniently blown down. It is all now dominated by the giant cooling towers, the pylons and the wire of the power station. Previous industry respected the scale of the gorge. This complex does not.

Here in the Ice Age, the waters of Severn were held back in a great sea, now named Lake Lapworth after the geologist who uncovered the evidence. Eventually the water forced its way through the carboniferous limestone to form the gorge. In so doing it laid bare coal, limestone, clay and ironstone, all the ingredients which were to make possible the industrialisation of the valley.

There were disadvantages in the instability of the banks, and in 1773 one of them surged into the river. John Wesley was staying at Madeley when, at four in the morning, he heard a rumbling noise, accompanied by "gusts of wind and wavings of the ground. Presently the earthquake followed . . . carried the barn about fifteen yards, and then swallowed it up in a vast chasm . . . It then moved under the bed of the river, which making more resistance, received a ruder shock, being shattered in pieces, and heaved up about thirty feet from its foundations. By throwing this and many oaks into its channel, the Severn was quite stopped up and constrained to flow backwards till, with incredible fury, it wrought itself a new channel. Such a scene of desolation I never saw. Will none tremble when God thus terribly shakes the earth?"

John Fletcher, the vicar of Madeley, printed his sermon on the event, describing how "a rock that formed the bottom of the river, has mounted up as a cork and gained a place on the bank, while a travelling grove has planted itself in the waters, and a fugitive river has invaded dry land." The scars of one of the landslides at Birches Coppice can still be traced.

Coal was mined here and charcoal used in the forges long before Abraham Darby arrived from Bristol in 1708. Within a year he was using Sir Basil Brooke's old furnace to smelt iron ore with coke. Everything stemmed from this innovation, and within twenty-five years of his arrival the place had been so transformed that his daughter was writing to her aunt about "the Stupendous Bellows . . . the mighty Cylinders, the wheels that carry on so many different branches of the work."

It was soon realised that a bridge was needed, and Abraham Darby III rebuilt the Old Furnace to accommodate the casting of what was to be the first iron bridge to cross the Severn. Wesley saw it before it was erected and was of the opinion that it weighed as much as the Colossus of Rhodes and would not soon be imitated. Richard Gough, in his 1789 edition of Camden's *Britannia*, described the ribs being cast in open sand, hoisted by ropes and chains onto a scaffold, and then lowered into place to be dovetailed and fastened together. The whole operation took only three months, and there were no accidents nor interruptions to river navigation. It was opened in 1781, and eighty years later was joined upstream by the Albert Edward Railway Bridge, cast and erected by the same company.

The Iron Bridge was a private toll bridge, with charges ranging from 2/- for every coach-and-six to one halfpenny for a pedestrian. There were no exceptions as the notice board made clear:"N.B. This bridge being private property, every Officer or Soldier whether on Duty or not, is liable to pay toll for passing over, as well as any baggage waggon, mail coach or the Royal Family."

Torrington thought it must be "the admiration as it is one of the wonders of the world." He visited Mr. Banks' iron furnace on the hillside and was shown "the astonishing progress of such (hellish hot) manufactories . . . Every cart belonging to this trade is made of iron, and even the ruts in the road are shod with iron." After the Iron Bridge, Coalbrookdale's most famous products were, probably, the four splendid gates for Hyde Park, which were first exhibited at the Great Exhibition in 1851.

Practically the whole area is now under the guardianship of The Ironbridge Gorge Museum Trust, with its information centre in the old toll-house and museum in the Great Warehouse. But the ironwork is not confined to the museum; it can still be seen in window-sills and frames, chimney-pots and railings.

The Iron Bridge.

The terraces of the labourers mingle with the more imposing homes of the iron-masters. Several were Quakers, and indeed, Abraham Darby's first link with the place was when he witnessed a deed, acquiring land for a Friends' burial ground at Broseley, some time before he moved here from Bristol. It was here that Elizabeth Gurney, who was to become Elizabeth Fry, was moved to become a Quaker and set out on the road of prison reform. Abraham Darby's son built the Meeting House at Coalbrookdale and was the first to be buried in the burial ground. The spiritual and intellectual life of other members of the community was cared for by the churches of St Luke and Holy Trinity, and the Coalbrookdale Literary and Scientific Institute, built in 1859.

Amongst the many industrial monuments are the Inclined Plane and the Tar Tunnel. The former was opened in 1793 and provided a speedy method of raising and lowering boats between the Severn and the terminus of the Shropshire Canal, two hundred feet up the cliff. The Tar Tunnel had been driven into the hillside six years earlier and took its name from the bitumen oozing from its sides. An Italian visitor was shocked by the state of the men working there, looking, he thought, like victims from Dante's Inferno, "so horribly disfigured and begrimed are they." But bitumen was valuable, not only for sale to boat builders, but as "bottled British Oil, a certain cure for Rheumatism."

The last of the industrial memorials is the Museum of the Coalport China Works. Jackfield, across the river from the Tar Tunnel, was known for its rich, darkly glazed earthenware in the early eighteenth century. Under John Rose the works were moved across the river and began to produce fine ware, much of it made famous by the Indian Tree pattern. In 1852 a new element was introduced when the brothers Maw moved to Benthall and began to make decorative tiles which they sold all over the world. They could be found in Battlefield Church, the Calcutta G.P.O., Lambeth Workhouse, Tokyo's Central Station, Balliol, *The Mountain Daisy* inn in Sunderland, Moscow's Public Baths, and the Pasha of Egypt's yacht.

Coalport Bridge, a wooden one in 1770, has been strengthened several times with cast-iron ribs, and has the date of one of these repairs, 1818, on the parapet. It leads to Broseley, famous for clay pipes and John Wilkinson, a man of radical views whose heart was reputed to be as hard as pig-iron. He was also something of a folk-hero after his death, for which he prepared his own epitaph, beginning, "Delivered from Persecution of Malice and Envy, here rests John Wilkinson, ironmaster, in certain hope of a better estate and Heavenly Mansion . . . His life was spent in action for the benefit of man, and . . . his different works that remain in various parts of the kingdom are testimonials of increasing labour."

The industries of the valley increased the prosperity of the surrounding countryside, farmers finding a ready market for animals and produce. When Torrington was in Broseley in 1784, it bore "all the marks of content, increase and riches." One hardly gets that impression today, even the delightful bracket on *Ye Olde Taverne* is without its sign. Camden commended a well here which burned "like the spirit of wine and brandy," but Broseley lacks the bustle of the crowds around the Ironbridge Gorge, and spirit seems to be missing.

Even so, it is a relief to leave the atmosphere of make-believe around Coalbrookdale and its museums, and to return to open country again. There is nothing dramatic about this stretch, the Severn flowing in a wide plain, and the villages standing back from the flood levels. Only the great houses venture near the river which meanders towards Bridgnorth between the Palladian Linley Hall and the Gothic Apley Park, a mile and a half apart and seventy years in time.

The church towers seen from the river are nicely varied and range from the Norman at Linley, Tudor at Sutton Maddock, Stuart at Stockton, and Victorian at Astley Abbots. The last-named, dedicated to St Calixtus, has a fine hammerbeam roof resting on animal corbels, and a rare Maiden's Garland. They usually consisted, as does this one, of a hoop, ribbons, gloves and a shield. They were carried by young children dressed in white at the head of the funeral procession of a girl. The gloves are supposed to represent a challenge to anyone questioning the dead girl's reputation, and the custom probably goes back before the Reformation. The shield in this case refers to the death, on May the 10th, 1707, of Hannah Phillips on the eve of her wedding. There is a collection of such garlands in the similarly named village of Abbots Ann in Hampshire.

Maiden's Garland, Astley Abbots.

CHAPTER THREE

Bridgnorth to Powick

THE Severn is joined by the Worfe before entering Bridgnorth, High Town on its sandstone cliffs towering over Low Town along the river below. They are linked by many flights of brick steps and the steepest cliff railway in the country. The town probably began as a fortified Saxon enclosure guarding a river crossing. It was taken over and refortified by Robert de Belesme, an unscrupulous Norman troublemaker who was eventually defeated and outlawed by Henry I. Bridgnorth was then given royal privileges and received its first charter in 1157.

As peace was established, its military importance declined and when Leland visited it he found many ruins; dwelling houses of timber in the castle grounds, and "the glory of the waulls . . . and the strength of the castle . . . decayed." There is now little of what Leland knew except part of the keep, leaning at a drunken angle as it was when Torrington, two hundred years ago, thought it was about to collapse.

Leland found nothing in Low Town except "a praty long strete of meane buildynge," whereas in High Town there was "one very fayre strete . . . going from Northe to Southe, and on each syde of the strete the howses be galeried; so that men may passe dry by them if it rayne." He attributed the town's poor appearance to a recession in the clothing trade, but in spite of this, it remained a place of some importance until the Civil War, when St Leonard's church, which was being used to store ammunition, caught fire. The flames spread quickly through High Town and great damage was done.

At the Restoration, Bridgnorth was rebuilt as a market centre, with a fine new Town Hall in the middle of the High Street and five important fairs. According to Richard Whitworth, writing in 1766, the fairs received about a thousand tons of cheese annually from Cheshire and Staffordshire. It arrived in waggons and was then shipped down the river by barge.

With the Town Hall, came the trappings of municipality, such as the borough maces, which can be dismembered so that the heads may be used as drinking vessels. The council also developed a complicated, almost Papal, method of choosing its bailiffs. According to an account written in 1739, fourteen burgesses were chosen as the selection committee, and having sworn that they would neither eat nor drink until they had reached a decision, they were locked up together until they had done so, "which hath often occasioned very long and tedious fastings even to the prejudice of their healths."

There is the usual ration of good pubs, a flamboyant Victorian market hall in multi-coloured brick, and a rebuilt North Gate which houses another of the Severn's splendidly traditional museums, a museologist's paradise. Completely unmodernised, it adds to the air of permanence which, traffic apart, one finds in Bridgnorth; a permanence appropriately symbolised by the stability of the leaning tower, and the posters of a firm of local estate agents called Doolittle and Dalley.

There are also two Anglican churches. St Leonard's was rebuilt after the fire and again in 1860, but now stands shut and forlorn in its cathedral-like precinct. It is surrounded by pleasant houses, the Palmers' Hospital, the Grammar School of 1629, and the timber-framed cottage where Richard Baxter lived as a curate. He ministered here, so he wrote, "to a dead hearted unprofitable people," much given to tippling and ill company; so he moved to Kidderminster where he found the congregation little better, but not quite "sermon-proof."

According to Doctor Johnson, who admired him, Baxter made it a rule to introduce something into every sermon he preached that was beyond the capacity of his audience to understand. That admirable practice was not always appreciated and he took to writing books. "Read any of them, for they are all good," said Johnson to Boswell; but Judge Jeffries did not agree: "Richard, thou hast written books enough to fill a cart; hadst thou been whipt out of thy writing trade forty years ago it had been happy."

St Leonard's is reached up a narrow lane containing eighteenth century almshouses, whereas St Mary Magdalene adorns the end of East Castle Street, with its wide brick pavements and gracefully curving range of elegant Georgian dwellings. The Governor's House and The Rectory frame the entrance to the church, which stands on the site of the castle chapel. It was built by Telford in 1792 and provides a superb end-piece to the town's best street, just as its simple dome acts as a suitable counterpart to the tower of St Leonard's. Huge, round-headed windows lighten the interior; there is a gallery with a bridge-like balustrade, and a new chancel with elaborate ironwork, added by Sir Arthur Blomfield in 1876.

Although Telford modestly claimed that the church's sole merit was "simplicity and uniformity," it was not well received. Henry Skrine found it too like a theatre, and later in the century, Samuel Smiles thought a Gothic building would have been more appropriate; "but Gothic was not then in fashion," he wrote, "only a mongrel mixture of many styles without regard to either purity or gracefulness." Many people nowadays would regard these as its most immediate qualities.

Bridgnorth Castle and Telford's Church.

East Castle Street, Bridgnorth.

The caves in the cliffs between High and Low Town were used by brewers to store Bridgnorth's famous Cave Ale. Below the cliffs the riverside suffers from the traffic, but the railings for the tow-ropes commemorate quieter days, when the town depended on trows and barges, rather than vans and lorries. Merchants from those earlier times gave Bridgnorth some of its finest houses. One such, Richard Forster, built one on the Cartway and inscribed it with the words, "Except the Lord BUILD the Owse the Labourers thereof evail nothing. Erected by R. For. 1580." It is now known as Bishop Percy's House, after the editor of *The Reliques* who was born in the town and lived here.

A Bridgnorth writer of another kind was Francis Moore. He was born in 1656, earned a living as physician, astrologer and schoolmaster, and became famous as the producer of *Old Moore's Almanac*. His first edition, *Kalendarium Ecclesiasticum*, was published in 1699 to promote the sale of some miraculous pills that he had invented. It confined itself to weather forecasting, but in 1700 he changed the title to *Vox Stellarum, being an Almanack for 1701*. He dedicated it to Sir Edward Acton, the Member for Bridgnorth and since that first issue it has, in every sense of the words, never looked back.

Bridgnorth was once called the Montpellier of England, and it is, perhaps, the least spoilt of the Severn towns. It has pleasing street furniture, good open spaces, the Severn Valley Railway, and fine country surrounding it. The six-arched bridge was built in 1823, replacing one which, in Leland's day, had "8 greate arches and a chapel of St. Sythe upon it." There was also at one time a prison over the gatehouse. The clock tower at the end of the bridge is a memorial to Rastrick and Trevithick, whose first locomotives were built in the ironworks here.

Downstream, Leland remarked on "some wylde ground by the way, and in some places good corne and grasse and . . . great plenty of wood whereof much cummithe down by Severne to serve the partes about Gloucester." Although there is no longer great plenty of wood, the rest applies, as the river curves towards Quatford, where it is turned by cliffs on which stands another church dedicated to Mary Magdalene.

Leland described its legendary foundation by Robert de Belesme's father, "at the desyre of his wyfe that made a vow thereof in a tempest on the se." The story tells how Adelissa, crossing from Normandy in a storm, was told by a priest that he had dreamed that they would all be saved if she would promise to build a church where the wild swine have shelter. There seems some doubt as to whether she came across any swine, but she certainly met her husband, and it seems to have been his decision to build the church on this natural defensive promontory. A town developed, and Quatford and Shrewsbury were the only Shropshire boroughs at the time of Domesday. But Adelissa's son, Robert, abandoned his mother's foundation and moved to a stronger site at Bridgnorth in 1100.

The river has now become commercialised, with chalets and caravans, and a Marina on Chelmarsh reservoir. The church of St Peter, high on a ridge above the water, has, like Quatford, a red brick tower and a mainly fourteenth century interior. Fixed to the wall of the porch, and bisected by a seat, is a primitive stone carving of the crucifixion. Dean Cranage thought it might have come from the churchyard cross, but if so it must have been a very large one. One of the bells, dated 1700, has its duties nicely summarised in the inscription:

> "I call the Quick and Dead
> Prepare to Church and Bed."

Quatt, on the east side of the river, is a more interesting settlement. It is primarily the estate village of Dudmaston, an eighteenth century mansion with grounds going down to the Severn and backed by what is left of the great forest of Morfe. The house, which has recently been given to the National Trust, contains a collection of seventeenth century flower pictures which once belonged to the Darbys of Coalbrookdale.

The village, which is well distanced from the house, has estate cottages, school, cricket pitch and handsome Dower House. The church has workmanship of high quality from mediaeval times to the late eighteenth century, and is very much the shrine of the Wolryches of Dudmaston. The lectern, in beautifully silvered oak, is carved with the names of the wardens and the date, 1629. The pulpit, of the same date, has around the top, "Preach the Word Be instant in Season Out of Season Reprove Rebuke Exhort," and around the base, "Crie aloud Spare not Lift up thy Voice like a Trumpet Tell the People of theyer Transgressions."

The noble monument of Francis Wolryche, with his wife, children and shrouded infant, has recently been regilded. He died in 1614, and the bodies of both husband and wife are tautly arched, as if straining to rise from their tomb. One of their children, George, who died in 1640, had his own last words placed on his memorial: "If in this Life onely there were hope in Christ wee were of all the most miserable. Verba morientis. Non but Christ. Non but Christ."

The Reverend G. J. Freeman visited Quatt in 1823 and disapproved of it. He called it a motley structure and deplored "an utter disregard of the taste and feelings of our forefathers. I never hear of a church undergoing repairs," he went on, "without trembling." His fears in many cases were amply justified, but not here, where the red brick tower and Georgian nave blend happily with the mediaeval chancel arch and arcade inside. According to Randall, wall paintings of the Last Judgement and the Seven Charities were revealed when the rebuilding was taking place.

The river continues in broad sweeps to Hampton Loade which once boasted a ferry, but now only an ugly footbridge and a station on the admirable Severn Valley Railway. A journey on this voluntarily operated line, which links Bridgnorth with Bewdley, is an excellent way of seeing this twelve mile stretch of the river. It keeps close to the bank for most of the distance, threading its way through a curious mixture of rich agricultural land, mining villages and holiday encampments.

Downstream, Alveley and Highley, each with attendant colliery, face one another across the river. Alveley church, whose Norman tower crowns a hill, was restored unmercifully in 1878. One of its curiosities is the north door, referred to in the parish guide as The Excommunication Door, with "X Dai of Juli 1545" carved on an oak beam above it. There is also a faded fifteenth century frontal and a richly coloured reredos, painted on zinc in the late nineteenth century.

The church at Highley also stands on a hill. There is good mediaeval ironwork on the door, a fine nave roof, and an unusual base to the churchyard cross. The village is disappointing except for a timber-framed house near the church and a well-kept station on the Severn Valley Line. The Borle Brook joins the river before it leaves Shropshire, a county of infinite variety, of curiously shaped hills and wide open valleys, of agriculture and industry, of Quaker ironmasters and hunting squires, of numerous villages and no large cities.

Upper Arley, another ancient ferry which has been replaced by an ugly bridge, was once part of Staffordshire and renowned for its vineyards and wine, "scarcely to be distinguished from the best French." It has now become a place to take the family, and the village has not quite adapted itself to their needs. An early, enlightened attempt to make use of its attractions was when Earl Mountnorris erected a tent on the river walk and encouraged families from the colliery villages to picnic here, away from their depressing environment.

St Peter's church is up a steep, attractive street at the top of the village. It has pleasantly curved communion rails, a cross-legged knight, and several florid memorials; one to the Honourable Henry Arthur Annesley, drowned one month after his wedding, not in the Severn, but at Blackpool. The station is one of the best on the line which, lower downstream, crosses the river by the Victoria Bridge. When it was built in 1861 it was the largest cast-iron arch ever constructed, twice as long as the Iron Bridge. Telford, who designed it, was lucky in the weather, a prolonged drought enabling him to raise it in a season, "as if by enchantment." The bridge was made by Sir John Fowler, the builder of the Forth Bridge in Scotland.

The valley then closes in as Wyre Forest and the Dowles Brook join it above Bewdley. Wyre, for three hundred years a hunting preserve of the Mortimers, now casts a small shadow of its former splendour. In Camden's day it was renowned for the remarkable height of its trees, and a few patches of its natural woodland may still be found amongst the newer plantations. Three famous trees, the Mawley and Goodmoor oaks and the Seckley beech, are witnesses to former greatness, while the Whitty pear has been called "one of the most highly documented trees in Britain." Not that its fruit was particularly desirable, being described in the mid-seventeenth century as "so rough as to be ready to strangle one."

There were many other varieties of pear growing in great abundance in Worcestershire, but Camden had no high opinion of the drink they produced, "a counterfeit wine called perry that is very much drunk, though it be, like other liquids of that kind, both cold and flatulent."* He had a more favourable view of the air and soil of the county, "so propitious, that it is inferior to none of its neighbours, either for health or plenty."

*Nevertheless the city of Worcester included three pears in its coat-of-arms.
Upper Arley.

Leland's is still the best description of Bewdley, which he called "the sanctuary town." It acquired this distinction when it was claimed by both Shropshire and Worcestershire. As neutral territory it remained a sanctuary for fugitives from both counties until it was allotted to Worcestershire in 1544. Leland described it, "set on the syd of an hill soe coningly that a man cannot wishe to set a towne better. It risethe from Severne banke . . . so that a man standinge on the hill trans pontem by est may descrive every howse in the towne, and at the rysinge of the sunne . . . the hole towne gliterithe, being all of new buyldinge, as it wer of gold." Leland may well have received this golden impression from the fine stone, quarried near Arley, which mellows to a honey colour with the passage of time.

Telford used it when he built the present bridge, and it has been its series of bridges which has been Bewdley's greatest asset. There was one in 1447 which was destroyed twelve years later. It was followed by a timber bridge until 1483, when "the goodly fayre bridge" which Leland used was built. It had five arches, and although it was damaged by flood in 1574 and by fighting during the Civil War, Habington still found it "a fayre brydge of stone emulating Worcester's brydge, with a gatehouse as Worcester's brydge, but thys of tymber, that towringe with stone."

It succumbed to the great flood of 1795. Thomas Bancks was on it when it began to break up: "The water was then running over the two ends, part of the fence walls on each side were washed away and the pavement in several places broke and fell into the river at the time I was upon the bridge." Within three years, Telford's fine structure, reputedly costing £9,000, replaced it. He fitted it with wooden rollers to prevent the bow-hauliers' ropes from chafing the stone, but the marks of ropes can still be detected on the underside.

It provides the axis to the town where, as in Leland's time, "there be but 3 streets memorable," Severnside, Load Street and High Street. Here many fine houses testify to its former prosperity: timber-framed ones side by side with others that have been refaced in Georgian brick, enhancing the wide streets and embellishing the river front.

The parish church was, for a long time, downstream at Ribbesford, and Leland knew only a small chapel-of-ease in Bewdley. Habington gave details of some elaborate glass in the church he visited. It depicted three dead people in their winding sheets, with underneath, the lines "Sucheas yee bin So weare we/As wee bin Shall ye bee./Take ye which of us three."

The present church, dedicated to St Anne, was built in 1745, though the tower is earlier. It was placed opposite the bridge at the top of Load Street, out of range of the river, but with no expectation of the flood of traffic passing it on either side today. The high Venetian windows face the bridge; inside, it is light and open, with galleries and huge Tuscan columns, and walls strangely bare of memorials.

Bewdley had acquired considerable control of the river trade by 1367 and was given its first charter by Edward IV in 1472, reputedly in return for services at the battle of Tewkesbury. One of its greatest assets was Wyre Forest, providing bark for the tanneries, charcoal for the forges, and timber for boats, brooms, baskets and houses. Drayton blamed Bewdley for destroying the forest and thought the townsfolk should have been ashamed "to behold her straight and goodly woods into the furnace sold." Habington was equally bitter about the way in which, until coal began to arrive by river, the town had been "sustayned by the utter overthrowe of a bosom frynde and nerest neyghboure, the late renowned forest of once flourishing Wyre."

The Bewdley boatmen had a reputation for ferocity and violence, and even religious differences sometimes led to hostilities. Richard Baxter disagreed publicly with John Tombes over infant baptism, and their supporters came to blows. Baxter was easily offended and Tombes, according to Aubrey, had a "curious, searching, piercing wit." He was an Anabaptist, and a contemporary recorded that their followers behaved "like two armies, about 1,500 a party, and truly at last they fell by the ears, hurt was done, and the Civil magistrates had much ado to quiet them."

When Richard Symonds was here during the Civil War he found that "the onely manufacture . . . is making of capps called Monmouth Capps, knitted by poore people for 2d a piece. Ordinary ones sold for 2, 3 and 4 shillings. First they are knit, then they mill them, then they work them with tassels, then block them, then they sheare them." Monmouth had lost its monopoly in the sixteenth century, and they continued to be made in Bewdley until, according to John Noake, "the present abomination . . . the French Hat was introduced." Apart from the decline in capping, Noake thought the arrival of the railway was the final blow to the town, because it killed the river trade and left the inhabitants with only three alternatives; to emigrate, to walk to work in Kidderminster, or to starve.

Randall agreed that the town in the 1860s looked as if it had seen better days, but found it "not without means of intellectual improvement; amongst others is the Load Street Institute." He may not then have been aware that Stanley Baldwin, Bewdley's other claim to fame, was being cosseted at Number 15, Lower Park. When he was born, he was "lifted" by his nurse, who always regarded his later success as proof of the efficacy of this ancient custom.*

Today, Bewdley is regarded by Pevsner as "the most perfect small Georgian town in Worcestershire." In its early days it benefited from the nearness of Tickenhill, one of Edward IV's royal manors. Leland went there and found it "standing in a goodly park, well wooded, on the very knapp of an hill." Mary Sidney, for whose amusement her brother wrote "Arcadia", was born here.

*Literally, the child was lifted towards the ceiling immediately after birth — it was believed that this would help it rise in the world.

Bewdley Bridge and Church.

The river, from Bewdley to Stourport, is thick with anglers, and the banks and verges even thicker with plastic bags, beer cans and litter. The Welsh Triads referred to the three defilements of the Severn; today they are innumerable and the materials from which they are made seem indestructible. The rubbish is at its worst near Ribbesford, a parish which was once more important than Bewdley, but which declined as Bewdley's prosperity increased. All that now remains, mercifully some distance from the disgraceful riverside, is a pleasant grouping of church, great house, farm and vicarage.

St Leonard's church was partly rebuilt in 1877 after it had been struck by lightning, but a good deal of the original building has survived, including the unusually massive fifteenth century timber arcade. Inside the porch, inscribed T M 1633 H W, is a Norman tympanum carved with an archer and animals. The pulpit is equally rural, with representations of a sow and her litter, a pig playing the bagpipes, and geese hanging a fox. There is a window at the west end, by Burne Jones, which is dedicated to Hannah Macdonald, a Methodist minister's wife and one of the country's most distinguished mothers. She had four daughters, one married Burne Jones, another Sir William Poynter, the third became Kipling's mother and the fourth the mother of Stanley Baldwin.

The church has every type of lighting, candles, oil lamps, floodlights, and a wide variety of monuments. These include coffin lids with crosses, a coloured memorial to "The Bayliffe of Bewdlie" (1626), and one to Helen Hopkins, who died during the Commonwealth:

> "Ask you in these what vertues were;
> Needless it is to write them here.
> Go ask the rich, they know full well;
> Go ask the poor for they can tell."

The steeply sloping churchyard has an even wider variety, ranging from the elegant calligraphy on the grave of "Johannes Humphredus V.D.M. philomath medicus," to a black marble slab bearing the arms of the Post Office Engineering Union (1978). Randall noticed the cast-iron cover to the tomb of the Bancks family (1788 - 97) with the stark warning: "Cursed be he that moves these bones."

Ribbesford House, beyond the church, is a large building of mixed descent. Leland called it "a good manour place" but the more cautious assessment of someone who had lived in it was that it was "pleasant for the somer but not healthful for the winter." It came into the hands of the Herberts who carried out alterations, but not enough for Lady Herbert who, in a letter in 1666, yearned for another staircase, "so that we neede not cary strangers by the buttery hach." It was used briefly by General de Gaulle and the Free French during the last war.

The river cliffs here contain caves which once harboured hermits. They were also put to other uses, as Bishop Latimer complained when he found the Redstone Rocks capable of holding five hundred men, "as ready for thieves and traitors as true men." In Habington's time there was still one hermit, and he was told that "many who traffycked on thys river gave as they passed by in theyr barges somewhat of theyre commodityes to thys hermit."

His hermitage contained a chapel with an altar, and other rooms "all formed out of the Rocke, yea the chimney rysinge steeple heghte thorough the stone ventethe the smoake to the overtoppinge hill." On the front of the cave were the arms of England, carved between those of Beauchamp and Mortimer. By the beginning of the nineteenth century, Cooke was complaining that the "present age has prophaned the seat of religious meditation by converting it into a cyder mill." When Noake visited it later, the community had increased to such an extent that it had its own cave school and alehouse.

Within four miles, the Severn is joined by the Stour, a tributary which, draining the industrial Midlands, has become one of its worst polluters. More beneficial was the Staffordshire and Worcestershire Canal, which would have gone to Bewdley if that town had shown any interest. Instead it was brought to the hamlet of Stourmouth. John Wesley was here six years after the canal had opened and could still refer to it as "a small new-built village." A year later he wrote: "Twenty years ago there was but one house here; now there are two or three streets, and as trade increases it will probably grow into a considerable town." He was proved right and Nash, writing a little later, noticed how a small alehouse in 1766 had become 250 houses and 1,300 inhabitants by 1795.

It is the Georgian houses of those first settlers, with the quays, warehouses and docks, which provide the most pleasing features of Stourport today; while the *Tontine Hotel*, built by the Canal Company in 1788, with terraces running down towards the river, is perhaps the most satisfying reminder of its former importance. The old bridge, which consisted of fifty-two arches, three of them over the river, was built in 1775 and was eventually destroyed by a flood. The present unimaginative structure was built in 1870, by which time the town was in decline, its prosperity reduced by the coming of the railway and the opening of the Birmingham and Worcester Canal. Randall found the town ruined and the *Tontine* almost empty. Yet in spite of what Noake called "its lack of genteel residences," it could well have become another Bewdley.

Instead it has been extensively and expensively municipalised; the vast, characterless Civic Centre overlooks a riverside stripped of its natural features and squandered on car parks, pleasure grounds and visitor attractions. Below the bridge, the canal basin and warehouses have been as effectively overwhelmed by a hideous, seemingly permanent, Fun Fair.

Stourport is overlooked from the west by the church of St Bartholomew at Areley Kings. On one of the walls of the large churchyard are the words

"Lithologema Quare Reponitur Sir Harry." The Greek, Latin and English words refer to Sir Harry Coningsby who was responsible for the repair of that wall of the churchyard. While playing with his small child, he let it fall from a window. It was killed and he retired to Areley where he was buried under a walnut tree which he had planted.

The church is late Victorian for the most part, but the tower belongs to a mediaeval building. The font, which was found under the floor during the restoration, has the inscription, "Tempore La-ammani santi," around its twelfth century base. Layamon was a priest who, in his own words, "dwelt at Ernleye, at a noble church upon Severn's bank — good it seemed to him there." He wrote a history of Britain in about 1200, and it has been assumed that Ernleye was Areley Kings.

There is a fine run of registers, beginning only three months after Thomas Cromwell had given orders in 1539 that such records should be kept. Under the chancel carpet is a memorial to Walter Walsh, who died at the age of eighty-three in 1702, "ruinated by 3 Quackers, 2 lawyers and a fanatick to help them."

Stourport.

The outskirts of the churchyard are graced by the handsome Jacobean rectory, complete with garden house to which Richard Vernon could retreat from domesticity. His arms and the inscription "Domesticis Richardi Vernon a rebus recessus" are in the gable. The Church House, which is timber-framed, and has served both as village school and coachman's house, looks out towards the Malverns and one section of the marvellous panorama that Areley Kings commands.

Shrawley, like Areley Kings, is high on a ridge above the river. "Thys Churche," wrote Habington, "mounted alofte on a hyll, seemethe a Lanterne of the Shyre." It is largely twelfth century except for the seventeenth century tower, and contains hatchments, numbered box pews, and Georgian Royal Arms. A verse, attributed to Wordsworth, commemorates Mary Vernon:

"Two babes were laid in earth before she died;
A third now slumbers at her mother's side;
Its sister-twin survives, whose smiles impart
A trembling solace to her father's heart."

A more robust verse has almost disappeared from a headstone near the porch. It shows a nicely carved figure of a gamekeeper with his dog. He is firing at a brace of birds, and below are the lines:

"No more with willing dog and gun,
To rise before the laggard sun;
No more before the social can,
Tomorrow's sport with joy to plan;
Death took his aim, discharged his piece,
And bade his sporting season cease."

There are more locks and weirs at Holt Fleet, once a hostelry famous for its tea gardens and picnics, now largely given over to caravans and their accessories. The bridge, another of Telford's (1828), leads to Ombersley, a model village which has benefited from the presence of the Sandys family at the Court. They played a leading part in the development of river navigation, and one of their number is reputed to have brought back from abroad the recipe with which William Perrins of Worcester produced his famous sauce.

Well away from Holt Fleet, and across a wilderness of gravel pits, lie Holt Castle and St Martin's church, a tranquil oasis in what looks like a lunar battlefield. The castle, a majestic house surrounded by yews and cedars, has a fourteenth century tower overtopping later additions. Habington, who rarely admitted to any difficulty in unravelling pedigrees, was bemused by the records here: "Coming to Holt I fall into a Labarinthe, knowing not which way to turn mee."

One of the most distinguished owners was Sir John Beauchamp, who was executed for high treason in 1388. He was Richard II's Steward of the Household and was beheaded after impeachment by the Merciless Parliament. He and his wife lie in the nave of Worcester Cathedral; she, with her head resting on a black swan whose neck is gracefully arched above her, he with his head on his swan helm, lying as if stricken, on its side.

Norman Font at Holt.

Across the road from Holt Castle, the Norman work in the lych gate is an introduction to the magnificent twelfth century carving on the doors and capitals of the church. The font is decorated with monstrous faces, linked mouth to mouth by trailing foliage, while fabulous beasts and grotesque heads decorate arches and pillars. The carving on the pulpit is more decorous, being the handiwork of the vicar's wife in Victorian times. Pevsner quotes the condescending remarks of a writer in *The Building News* in 1858: "We refuse to criticise them, as they are the work of a lady, and it is pleasing to find them taking an interest in these matters."

The river turns south to Grimley, a place-name which, according to Ekwall, means "a wood haunted by a spectre." The village contains the remains of a Roman fort, a heavily restored Norman church, and Thorngrove, once the refuge of Napoleon's brother, Lucien. He married the widow of a stockbroker, and Napoleon offered him the Kingdom of Naples if he would give her up. He refused, tried to escape to America, was captured by the British, and allowed to settle at Thorngrove for which he paid £9,000.

Bishop Hooper was born here, and Sir Samuel White Baker, the African explorer, is buried here. He lies beside "his second devoted wife," Florence. Baker was educated in Gloucester and first married a daughter of the vicar of Maisemore. He is said to have bought the intrepid girl who became his second wife in a Turkish slave market. She accompanied him fearlessly on all his great journeys, and no matter what he paid for her, no man ever got a better bargain. She died in 1916.

Grimley leads to Hallow, and Noake describes its chapel in 1830 as being, "of that peculiar character of which even a congregation of Primitive Methodists would now be ashamed." The present commandingly ornate church was built forty years later. The village once boasted a purgative spring, said to be a mixture of Epsom and Glauber salts, which rivalled any Cheltenham concoction. But Hallow's main claim to fame was its park.

Leland described it as "a Park without a Howse," which was used by the monks of Worcester when they wished to escape to higher ground, where they would be "no waye annoyed with the contagion vaporing from the water," which troubled them nearer the city. It had the added attraction of being covered with sweet-smelling mint, so that when Queen Elizabeth I went hunting there, "she gave it an extraordinary commendation, a deynty situation scarce second to any in England."

And Hallow has not yet been entirely engulfed by Worcester, a town which grew up around the lowest Severn ford to be unaffected by the tide and bore. From the Iron Age until the Roman occupation the crossing was guarded from the ridge above the river, and Habington looked upon Roman Worcester as defending the very "skyrtes of theyre Empire."

Wesley found it one of the liveliest places in England, and it has tended to display an active, and sometimes ruthless, independence ever since a mob murdered two of Harthacnut's tax-collectors when they were hiding in the cathedral. On that occasion Worcester was destroyed, though the citizens escaped to Bevere Island where they successfully withstood the whole English army. The town was rebuilt, and by the time of Domesday there was a motte and bailey castle, four churches and a community boasting 131 burgesses. It received its first charter in 1189 and was soon to be described as "a well composed corporation and a well governed city."

When Leland arrived, the walls with their six gates were in good repair and, although the castle was "clene down", there were "dyvers fayre strets in the towne, well buyldyd with tymbar." Together with the cathedral there were eight parish churches, while the bridge was "a royal peace of worke, high and stronge and hath six great arches of stone." Habington confirmed the splendour of that bridge, "bewtifyed and streangthened with a fayre towre." He also named some of the streets: Huckster Street, Goosethrottle Lane, Glovers Street, Needelers Street, Mealecheaping and Leach Street, "the street of death, leadynge to the Pryories great churchyard, wheare not only the whole citty but allso other adjoyninge villages interred then the bodyes of the departed."

Leland attributed Worcester's prosperity to cloth: "The welthe of Worcester standithe most by draping and noe town of England at this present tyme maketh soe many cloathes yearly as this towne doth." Habington thought the broadcloth so exceedingly fine that no one had ever worn the like, and he described visitors to the town's fairs as more like pilgrims than merchants for "when they saw a far off but the topps of the steeples, they presently on theyre knees fall to theyre prayers." The reputation did not last, and Cooke's *Topographical Guide* at the beginning of the nineteenth century attributed the decline of the cloth trade "to the frequently detected cheats of the manufacturers," which may, of course, be what those early pilgrims were praying to be saved from.

Worcester was involved several times in the Civil War, and the second Duke of Hamilton, who was wounded leading a charge and died in the Commandery, is buried near the high altar of the cathedral. But as with so many English towns, the setbacks were temporary, and Symonds in his diary describes a flourishing community led by mayor, sheriff, coroners, recorder, town clerk, six aldermen, twenty-four grand councillors and forty-eight common councillors, "all in purple faced with sathan."

Doctor Johnson found it "a very splendid city," and most visitors approved of the inhabitants, although one eighteenth century antiquary would only go so far as to say that "they are seldom addicted to vices of an enormous nature." Defoe thought it well populated, rich and full of business, but not well built, the houses close and old, and the civic accommodation not worth attention, "unless it be how much it wants to be mended." This situation was to improve, and, before Defoe's tour was published, Thomas White had embarked upon the exquisite Guild Hall which bears his signature, and the date 1722, amidst the trophies on the pediment. The central section has a statue of Queen Anne who is flanked by Charles II and Charles I holding a model of the cathedral. White, who was a pupil of Sir Christopher Wren, also produced the figure of Britannia on the house of the headmistress of The Alice Ottley School.

During that same century Worcester acquired four fine Georgian churches, and when Torrington arrived he could find little to criticise except, inevitably, his lodgings at *The Hop Pole*, "a noisy, dear inn." He perambulated "a well built, well paved town . . . and walked over the new bridge which has lately been finished and is the best town bridge we have ever seen." It was built by John Gwynne after completing the bridge at Atcham. He placed Sabrina's head over the central arch and gave it two elegant toll houses.

Gwynne, who was born in Shrewsbury, started life as a carpenter, and then began to write books on design and architecture. He became a friend of

The Guildhall, Worcester (1722). ▶

Doctor Johnson, and Boswell knew him as "a fine, lively, rattling fellow," adding that Johnson "kept him in subjection, but with a kindly authority." Gwynne's most important book was *London and Westminster Improved*, in which he urged that London should be planned as a whole and not be developed piece-meal. He was given the freedom of Worcester in 1783 and three years later was buried in the graveyard of St Thomas' Hospital.

Torrington listed Worcester's manufactures as carpets, gloves and china. Nelson who, like Torrington, stayed at *The Hop Pole,* approved of the china and ordered a large amount from Chamberlain's works, but was furious with "those damned glove women" for disdaining Lady Hamilton. John Wesley, who looked with affection on "our lovely and loving people of Worcester, plain, old genuine Methodists," would have approved of the glove women.

Cobbett, who was here in 1826, found Worcester, "one of the cleanest, neatest and handsomest towns I ever saw. Indeed, I do not recollect to have seen any one to equal it . . . and the people are, upon the whole, the most suitably dressed and most decent looking . . . The town is precisely in character with the beautiful and rich country, in the midst of which it lies."

It is unfortunate that the planners and councillors of the present century have decided to put it in character, not with its beautiful countryside, but with the motor car; and to have disembowelled it in order to produce a disastrous haemorrhage of fast, endlessly flowing traffic. Worcester, more than any other town, managed to preserve its links with the past during the revolutionary changes of the eleventh century, and as recently as 1920, A. G. Bradley could still call the city "compact and undefiled." The saintly Bishop Wulfstan, weeping as he watched Norman developers demolishing his Anglo-Saxon minister, admitted, "We miserable people have destroyed the work of saints, pompously thinking we can do better." It is a pity there has been no such compunction amongst the city's more recent developers.

One thing that has survived the muddled, middle years of this century is the river embankment which, on the right bank between the bridge and Diglis, provides splendid views of the Cathedral from an unexploited path where pedestrians and anglers can find peace. Habington described the view in the seventeenth century: "Thus standeth Worcester, pleasantly mounted on an easy ascendinge hyll rysinge from the Eastern bancks of Severn." With the Cathedral at the centre it is still a memorable prospect.

The Cathedral's external veneer is uncompromisingly Victorian; inside it is very different. The later restoration was by Scott and even he was well aware, as he pointed out in a letter to Canon Wood, that "Worcester enjoys an unenviable notoriety for the destruction of its antiquities." So he moved cautiously, and the interior has retained, almost entirely, its thirteenth century splendour; while down in the early Norman crypt the chronological growth of the building is discreetly exhibited.

King John was a visitor in 1206 and asked in a codicil to his will to be buried here. It has been suggested that he may have been influenced by an earlier prophecy, attributed to Merlin, that he would be placed amongst the saints. Certainly, he lies between the tombs of St Oswald and St Wulfstan, and his Purbeck marble effigy rests between the heads of these bishops. Defoe was told that the surrounding sanctity was expected to give him much needed assistance at the last trump. The tomb was opened in 1797, and "Oh! what a treat for the Antiquarian," exclaimed the sexton, when it was found that as a further precaution, the King had been buried in a monk's cowl, "as a passport through the regions of Purgatory."

As with Edward II at Gloucester, John's presence was an asset to the Cathedral, not only through the gifts of pilgrims, but by the return of ground which had once been confiscated from the monastery.

Appropriately in the birthplace of Hannah Snell (1723-1792), the woman soldier wounded twelve times on active service, there are some fine military memorials. The most dramatic is the huge marble effigy of Sir Henry Walton Ellis, being caught by an angel brandishing an iron wreath, as he falls from his horse in the moment of victory at Waterloo. More restrained is the memorial to those who fell by the Sutlej River in 1845/6.

The arts are represented by Elgar, who was born three miles outside the town, Mrs Henry Wood, born here but buried in Highgate cemetery, Mrs Sherwood, the author of *The Fairchild Family*, Prebendary James, remembered as "a Scholar and a ripe good one", and Dr John Hough who, "called forth to the dangerous and important station" of President of Magdalen College, Oxford, fell foul of James II. To his courage in opposing "The Rage of Popish Superstition and Tyrany," his epitaph proclaims, "let the Annals of England tesify." Roubiliac's huge monument shows the bishop soaring heavenward, against a background of Magdalen trying to eject him while he refuses to hand over the keys. It is comforting to find lower down the monument, that in spite of academic perils, "he expired without a groan" at the age of ninety-three.

Other episcopal memorials, and there are a good many more than at Gloucester, range from Nollekens' bust of Bishop Johnson, who was run over by a waggon in Bath, to the delightfully unpretentious tomb of Bishop Bullingham, supporting on his stomach a massive stone with the words:

"Here born Here Bishop Buried here
A Bullingham by name and stock
A man twice maried in Godes Fear
Chief pastor late of Lincolns flock
Whom Oxford trained up in yowthe
Whom Cambridge Doctor did create
A painful preacher of the truthe
He chayng'd his life for Happiest state
    18 April 1576."

It would have helped the verse if only he could have lived for another two years.

Worcester Cathedral.

The Royal Arms in the north aisle are seventeenth century; but in Habington's time they were those of Queen Elizabeth and adorned the choir, as did the magnificent organ case, decorated with royal badges and the arms of those who had contributed to its cost. It was inscribed: "By the meditation and mediation of Thomas Tomkins, Organist heere unto the Right reverend Bishop and Venerable Deane who gave theise munificent guiftes and invited their fryndes by the industry of the said Thomas Tomkins." He was organist from 1596 to 1646.

The Cathedral Library contains, in the Worcester Antiphonar, one of the few collections of liturgical music to escape destruction when Edward VI's Prayer Book was introduced. It includes music going back to the thirteenth century and, mercifully, remained undiscovered when the bishop ordered a great bonfire on College Green to dispose of all the old service books.

Although the Cathedral dominates the town, Worcester has many good parish churches: All Saints, with its fine sword rest, and the chandelier presented by a Quaker in return for being excused his parish duties; St Swithun's, with its impressive pulpit and mayoral chair; the spire of St Andrew's and the facade of St George's. And in quite a different category, the Friends Meeting House of 1700, in a simple inconspicuous cottage.

Several of the churches seem to be going out of use but their towers and spires still add variety to the sky line, which is more than can be said for domestic buildings. The magnificent timber-framed Greyfriars and the Commandery, both from the fifteenth century, remain, as does the Berkeley Hospital from the eighteenth. Occasional buildings such as Victoria House, which was once *The Hop Pole*, or Number 61 Broad Street, tall and slender with Venetian windows and a hidden belvedere from which to view the scenery, shine like good deeds in a naughty world.

One of Worcester's curiosities has been the success of its porcelain industry. None of the ingredients of china are found locally, and as a result the raw materials had to be obtained from Cornwall, Sweden, France and America. The craft was introduced as a substitute for the declining cloth trade, and in spite of difficulties, famous firms, such as Flight and Barr, prospered and carried the city's name across the world. Many of their products can be seen in the Dyson Perrins Collection at The Royal Worcester Porcelain Works.

At Diglis the river divides around the island, the western branch going over the weir, and the eastern passing the locks and docks around the basin of the Birmingham canal. The Severn is then joined by the Teme, a tributary which once owed allegiance to the Wye, and changed course in the last twenty thousand years. It is crossed by a fine fifteenth century bridge, leading to Powick, a fashionable suburb which Torrington likened to Clapham.

The large church has an enormous Royal Arms in the entrance. There is also a charming memorial by Thomas Scheemakers to Mary Russell, an amateur musician who died in 1786. The text praises her "instrumental harmony" and a roundel shows her teaching music to a small child. A later musician to be associated with Powick was Elgar. One of his first appointments was in 1879 when he became instructor to the Powick Lunatic Asylum Band. Even such a curious position as that did not affect his deep love for this stretch of the river, and for many years he harboured the hope that one day he might be buried close to the delectable spot where Teme and Severn meet.

CHAPTER FOUR

Kempsey to Gloucester

THERE are no bridges between Worcester and Upton and in emergencies like the Civil War temporary constructions resting on boats had to be used. The Commonwealth forces crossed the Severn below its junction with the Teme in this way, before launching one of their attacks on Worcester. The country is flat, dominated from the west by the Malverns, and is notable for the size of its churches.

One of the largest is at Kempsey, another Worcester dormitory which Noake called "a favourite place for genteel families, officers, elderly ladies and tradesmen to retire to." It is a long village with several Georgian and timber-framed houses to grace the traffic pouring down the main street. St Mary's church, high above the brook, in a huge churchyard, has a magnificent chancel. It was built in the thirteenth century when Walter de Cantelupe was both bishop of Worcester and lord of the manor of Kempsey. In many ways a much greater bishop than his nephew, Saint Thomas of Hereford, he is reputed to have said mass for Simon de Montfort and the captive Henry III before the battle of Evesham. The King and de Montfort slept in the manor house, as did Edward I on a later occasion, after travelling by boat from Worcester.

The Cantelupe leopards' heads can be seen over the sedilia in the church, and there is a noble east window containing good mediaeval glass. Like so many churches in this diocese, it has been comprehensively scraped, and like Ross-on-Wye it was renowned, not for its chancel, but for a tree growing inside. A chestnut, confiscated from a choirboy, is said to have been carelessly cast against the tomb of Sir Edmund Wylde, where it took root. The tomb, which dates from 1620, is one of the few early monuments in the church, and Sir Edmund's effigy is surmounted by an arch bearing carvings of his sword and helm.

The churchyard looks down on the Ham, which has good views of the Malverns, and was once the scene of a duel between Sir John Parkington, later Secretary of State for War, and the master of the Worcestershire Hunt, who accused him of getting too close to the hounds. It took place in 1827, without anyone being hurt.

The Malverns from Kempsey.

Across the river, the red brick church at Callow End plays second fiddle to the high, striped, Italianate tower of Stanbrook Abbey, both of them built in the 1880s. The river, which here runs in unusually long straight stretches, is eventually turned by the rocks below Rhydd; a Welsh place-name meaning a ford, so possibly a crossing once used by the drovers.

The steep banks of Cliffey Wood give way to open meadows as the river nears Severn Stoke. This was a village which interested Cobbett because the parson owned a peculiar hot-house for raising grapes. It is close to the river and the church has suffered from flooding on many occasions. It was restored, with sombre cement on its stripped walls, after three feet of water had covered the floor in 1890. But it has a Norman tower and a communion flagon hall-marked 1619, which is engraved with a picture of Christ the Good Shepherd, dressed in contemporary seventeenth century clothes.

Noake retails a legend of how Mr Wybrough, the minister of Severn Stoke, was shot in the pulpit by Mr Somers, the father of the famous Lord Chancellor:

"His satanical zeal at Stoke it was such
That he shot at the parson; you'll think it too much
But he loved the Old Cause as his son loves the Dutch."

There is now a good deal of expensive housing in a village which Habington called, "well seated by the River Severn." But the Benefaction board in the church recalls the less inflationary days of 1783 when a donation of £10:15: 6 was enough to build a pair of new houses, to replace two which had been destroyed by fire.

Hanley Castle, on the west bank, has given its name to the village. But only the moat remains of the great castle which was built by King John, where the Duke of Warwick was born, and where, twenty years later, he died. Leland called it an uplandish town, a flight shot from the Severn, but found that the keeper of the park in which the castle stood had "clene defacid it." When Habington visited it he found only "a lytell rubbyshe and a seely barne to teach us that the glory of the World vanishethe to nothinge."

The village has a small green, a cedar tree, timber-framed almshouses and grammar school, a pub, and several elegant Georgian houses. The church, a satisfying mixture of Norman stone and Stuart brick, was the mausoleum of the Lechmeres, a distinguished family which included a number of Members of Parliament. One of the more important was Nicholas, born in 1675, and of "a temper, violent, proud and impracticable." He decided to make a speech immediately after taking the oath when he was admitted to Parliament. It was objected to on the grounds that, as he had not sat down, he was not a sitting Member. His father, a supporter of the Commonwealth, had walked in Cromwell's funeral procession.

Rhydd.

The Lechmeres built Severn End, nearer the river, after the castle had disappeared, but a fire in 1896 destroyed much of that late-seventeenth century house. It was renowned for its many passages and staircases, and still holds the Lechmere Stone, part of a small tombstone, carved with the figure of Christ on one side, and a round-headed cross on the other. It probably dates from the ninth century.

Upton-on-Severn is a town which has depended greatly on its bridges. In Leland's time, when it was the only one between Worcester and Gloucester, it was of wood and, by 1599, had so decayed that it was "not sufficient for passengers to pass." A new one in 1605 seems to have been of stone, and was commended by Celia Fiennes when she crossed it a hundred years later. But arguments over responsibility for its upkeep meant that it had to be replaced twice before the present bridge was built in 1939.

The river is narrower here than at Bewdley, and the waterside lacks that town's spaciousness. Nor is it as well planned, and the marina, the boats, the caravans and the holiday crowds seem to disorganise it. It is all very different from the scene a hundred years ago when the fields along the river were bright with Meadow Saffron, and the marshy hollows with drifts of Water Lily and Water Violet.

There are some good houses along the riverside and handsome inns in the town, especially *The Talbot* and *The White Lion*. Torrington stayed at the former in 1781 and at the latter in 1787. He could not understand why Fielding placed so much of *Tom Jones* in such a topographically unsuitable place as Upton, nor why he could introduce "such an improbability as Tom Jones calling for champagne in such an inn."

Upton.

The old church, on its central mound, has been pulled down except for its fourteenth century tower, which was crowned in the eighteenth century with Anthony Kek's distinctive wooden cupola. Noake, who thought it looked incongruous, says that it cost £275; but it is an engaging landmark and compliments the fine steeple of the new church built by Sir Arthur Blomfield in 1878. Even so, and in spite of the municipal tidying up, the old church seems sadly neglected by all but the pigeons today. Disgracefully, the tombstones have been dismembered to make pavements, steps and, worst of all, crazy-paving.

When Leland was here he commented on a stable belonging to the King, "a late occupied by great horses." It was pulled down in the reign of Charles II, and a house known as The King's Stable replaced it. Many years later Cobbett came to stay with his friend John Price across the bridge at Ryall, and found Upton famous, not for horses, but for Hereford cattle and Leicester sheep. "The animals," he wrote, "seemed to be made for the soil and the soil for them."

What worried him was that so much of the meat the valley produced went to Cheltenham, a place he loathed; where "East India plunderers, West India floggers, English tax-gorgers, together with gluttons, drunkards and debauchees of all description, female as well as male, resort, at the suggestion of silently laughing quacks in the hope of getting rid of the bodily consequences of their manifold sins and iniquities." Fosbrooke, writing at the same time, was more concise when he referred to Cheltenham's reliance on "the dissipation trade."

If Cheltenham has changed, the Severn has remained the same, flowing unhindered through wide meadows, past the dismantled railway at Saxon's Lode (originally Sexton's), and the ferry at Ripple, to the slender viaduct which now carries the M 50 over the valley.

Ripple was a village on the coach road between Tewkesbury and Worcester, renowned for its perry and notorious for the rapacity of its fishermen. And it certainly seems to have prospered, with a splendid Georgian rectory, a large church, and a pleasant mixture of half-timbered and brick houses around the cross. When Noake was here he visited the church and commented on "carved oak painted to imitate oak, good masonry stuccoed to imitate masonry;" but it has now been stripped of its plaster and the masonry defined in cement. The steeple was damaged by lightning in 1583 and it was not until 1713 that the present heightened tower replaced it.

In spite of the restoration, the thirteenth century chancel is large and light and harbours a famous series of misericords. They depict, month by month, the labours of the farming year; wood-gathering, hedging and ditching, sowing, bird scaring, blessing the crops, hawking, baking, harvesting, malting, pig feeding, pig killing and, in December, sitting by the fire to spin.

There are four more, illustrating the blessings of the sun (light and warmth), the moon and the constellation of the Water Carrier.

The east window, which now contains Victorian glass, was once alight with the arms of Henry V and other members of his family. The shattered remains of that fifteenth century glass, along with a rare latten censer, were found when digging a grave below the altar in 1734. The chancel still contains a brass to John Woodward, "sometime Yeoman of the Gard unto King Phillipe and allso to Queen Elizabeth." He died in 1596 and was joined by his grandson William, "who was laid down to sleep with his grandfather in the dust of the same grave" in 1668.

There is a huge iron-bound chest, nearly nine feet long, and the Royal Arms of George I. According to Noake, the room over the porch was used by the parson to hang his game. It is certainly an eighteenth century addition, but can hardly have been constructed solely for that purpose.

Ripple was the scene of the last Royalist victory in the Civil War, when Waller was defeated by Prince Maurice and driven back towards Tewkesbury. The noise of that battle can have been but a whisper to the uproar where the M 5 and M 50 meet just east of the village.

It was a large parish and included chapels across the river at Holdfast and Queenhill. Habington went to Holdfast and found it "so dangerously deformed with ruines as I scarcely durst look into it, yet I saw painted on the South wall of the body thereof a young Kinge ryding on a red lyon, the history or mistery thereof I know not." The other chapel at Queenhill has survived, isolated by the M 50, but beautifully situated above the valley.

It is a church with interesting monuments, starting with the Elizabethan Henry Ffeeld, incised between his two wives, one of whom wears a bowler hat with a wavy brim, and culminating with the almost indestructible Lt-Colonel W. L. Herford, C.B., of The Royal Welsh Fusiliers. After carrying the regimental colours at the landing in Egypt in 1801, he fought at Copenhagen, Martinique and the Peninsula. He was wounded at Albuera, "where he received a rifle shot through the calf of his leg, and a musket ball in the right breast which was extracted from the back, having passed through the lungs." He lost no time in returning to duty and the command of the regiment at Orthez and Toulouse, and died at the age of sixty-eight in 1845.

There is some good fourteenth century glass, including the arms of England before Edward III quartered the arms of France in 1340; and the figure of St Anne, teaching the Virgin to read from a book, open at the letters A, B, C.

On the right bank, and still in Worcestershire, the grey chalk tower of Bushley church marks the centre of the Dowdeswell estates. It was built by Blore for the Reverend E. C. Dowdeswell in 1843. Noake, highly critical of anything he considered unorthodox, thought "some of the furniture and accessories would probably have the effect of alarming sensitive minds," but found nothing in the services to demand condemnation, "except that the minister preached in a surplice."

It was a famous parish for its picnics and harvest suppers. "Squire Dowdeswell," wrote Noake, "not only owns the entire parish, but rules over it with the mild benignity of a constitutional sovereign." Which was appropriate in a family that included a commander-in-chief in India, who was also one of the first great print collectors, and an eighteenth century Chancellor of the Exchequer. The long inscription to the latter, written by Burke, assures us that, "immersed in the greatest affairs, he never lost the antient, native, genuine English character of a Country Gentleman."

Squire Dowdeswell used the same architect, Blore, to build Pull Court, now Bredon School. It is Jacobean in character, with grounds attributed to Capability Brown, and an artificial ruin which contains mediaeval windows from the old church.

What Habington called "the greatest water ornament of our Shire" now leaves his beloved Worcestershire, "bestowing such benefitte on every side as it passeth on in a slow course towards the South there to impart the like bountie to Gloucestershire." Nowadays, for about two miles, from Bushley to the weir at Tewkesbury, the Severn forms the boundary between the two counties. Then Gloucestershire takes over completely.

It is a county of which Marshall wrote: "The eye must be dim and the heart benumbed which can be insensible to its rural beauty." And Mrs Craik, the author of *John Halifax Gentleman*, described this stretch of the Severn as neither grand nor striking, but calm, generous, gracious, "rolling through the land slowly and surely, like a good man's life, and fertilizing wherever it flows."

The Mythe Bridge, Tewkesbury.

Before being joined by the Warwickshire Avon, the river passes under the Mythe Bridge, built by Telford in 1826 to replace a ferry. Telford reckoned it the handsomest bridge that had been built under his direction: "Looking therefore at this bridge, over such a fine navigable river, passing through a beautiful valley, at a proper distance from an ancient town . . . and having the Malvern Hills in the distance, it seems not presuming too much to assert, that the picture will not suffer by comparison with any other which can be selected." It has a pleasant toll house, flood arches on the approaches, and it cost nearly double the estimate of £20,000.

The main Tewkesbury bridge was over the Avon where it divides into two branches. Leland described it as "a great bridge of stone" and noticed that, although King John had ordered that it should be maintained out of the market tolls, the money was, in fact, being retained by the town.

The northern branch of the Avon flows into the Severn above Upper Lode, where locks, a weir and islands have divided the main stream. The southern branch has been diverted closer to the town and joins the Severn at Lower Lode. Severn Ham is thus enclosed by water, and forms a huge open expanse between Tewkesbury and the river. The quays have been used for the transferring of cargoes between the two rivers, and around the Abbey and Borough Mills the river is colourful with long flour barges, bearing the names of Severn villages, like Tirley, Chaceley and Apperley.

Building in Tewkesbury has been conditioned by the flooding of its rivers, and the consequent richness of the surrounding water meadows. So the town plan has changed little since Leland described the three streets meeting at the Cross. As a result, Tewkesbury is still Y-shaped and constricted. This has led to much background building, down alleyways and behind the major streets, and it was in these crowded quarters that one of the town's occupations, stocking-making, flourished. Mrs Craik remembered "The drowsy burr of many a stocking-loom coming through the open doors, the prattle of children paddling in the gutter and sailing thereon a fleet of potato parings."

Camden, who called it "a large fair town," noted that it was famous for its mustard, but it was also an important centre for the leather and malting trades. The latter is commemorated in *The Royal Hop Pole Hotel*, where Mr Pickwick and his companions consumed bottled ale, madeira and port before continuing their journey. The bridges made Tewkesbury a busy coaching station and this increased the number and importance of its inns.

There are still many fine timber-framed houses such as *The Bell Hotel, The Black Bear Inn,* and the Abbey Lawn Cottages, recently restored by a local trust; but the Mythe brick works which were operating in the seventeenth century, led to some houses being refaced in brick. So the age of buildings is most easily considered from the back. The High Cross, where the Lancastrian prisoners were executed after the battle in 1471, was demolished in 1650 and the site is now appropriately occupied by the War Memorial.

The Avon Bridge, Tewkesbury.

There was a castle at Tewkesbury called Holme, south-west of the Abbey, and Leland traced a few of its foundations; but for most of its history the town has been dominated by the massive Romanesque tower of what Defoe called "the largest private parish church in England." It achieved that stature because the townspeople, to their eternal honour, bought the Abbey from the King at the Dissolution. They paid the large sum, for those days, of £453, said to have been the estimated value of the bells and the lead roof. Although the nave was not used, it was saved from destruction, and the great church still stands almost complete, enclosed by fine trees and the spendid gates given by Lord Gage in 1734.

It was consecrated in 1121 and thereafter increased in splendour under a long line of illustrious benefactors, De Clares, Beauchamps, Despensers, as well as local citizens. Until the fourteenth century it was almost the twin of Gloucester's abbey church. Both were then remodelled, Gloucester on account of the droves of pilgrims to the tomb of Edward II, and Tewkesbury through the influence and wealth of Edward's favourite, Hugh le Despenser.

It would be presumptuous to do more than list some of the beauties of this magnificent building; the high altar dedicated in 1239; the fourteenth century vaulting of the Presbytery with the great bosses added in celebration of the Yorkist victory in 1471; the chantry of Edward Despenser, with the knight kneeling on the roof and praying towards the altar; the tomb of Edward III's standard bearer at Crecy; the alabaster effigies of Hugh le Despenser and his wife Elizabeth; the sacristy door, strengthened with strips of armour from the battlefield; the Armada chest; the Beauchamp Chapel; the chancel windows; Queen Anne's Royal Arms; and Flaxman's monument to Lady Clarke who is commended for being, "as a Christian, remarkably pious and charitable." The Abbey is probably unique in possessing a Communion flagon, hallmarked 1660, which was presented by the bachelors and virgins of the parish, "Coelibum et virginium Oblatio . . . "

The church is also rich in organs. The Milton organ was built in Elizabeth's time for Magdalen, Oxford. The college presented it to Cromwell, who placed it in Hampton Court where it may, or may not, have been played by Milton. It was returned to Magdalen in 1660 and sold to Tewkesbury in 1737. The case is one of the most beautiful in England, with pipes superbly embossed and gilded. There is also an early nineteenth century chamber organ, and another made for the South Kensington Exhibition of 1885.

But while the Abbey, with its mills, its gatehouse, its Barton and Abbey House, dominate the town, Nonconformity was also influential. The Baptist Chapel, built in 1623, is one of the oldest in Gloucestershire; and in 1676, three-quarters of the population were reckoned to be Nonconformist. *The Tudor House Hotel* once harboured a Dissenting Academy, and John Wesley waded through deep flood water to preach at what he considered, "the liveliest place in the circuit." On later visits he complained that the meeting house was much too small to hold the congregation.

The Abbey Tower, Tewkesbury.   The Abbey Gates, Tewkesbury.

Lastly, Tewkesbury may be remembered for the fortuitous part it played in the protection of old buildings. In 1864 Sir Gilbert Scott estimated that £15,000 was needed for repairs to the Abbey. He began restoration in 1875 and a progress report in *The Builder* caught the eye of William Morris, whereupon he dashed off his controversial letter asking if it was too late to save the Abbey from destruction by Scott. More important, he suggested the setting up of a body to protect ancient buildings from religious, artistic and historical enthusiasts who, he claimed, had done more damage in a few years than all the previous centuries of revolution, violence and neglect together.

As a result, the Society for the Protection of Ancient Buildings was formed, and nicknamed by Morris himself, "The Anti-Scrape." By then the restoration of the Abbey was well under way, and another article in *The Builder* was casting doubt on the wisdom of using black mortar to repoint the masonry. This would still be one of the chief criticisms of Victorian restorers, not only in the Severn valley but throughout the country.

It is, however, appropriate that a town which played a part, unwitting though it may have been, in the protection of ancient buildings, should have restored so admirably the fifteenth century Abbey Lawn cottages.

Forthampton, a rambling village of black and white houses, lies on the road to Lower Lode, once a ferry which Richard Dowdeswell managed to persuade Parliament to exempt from tolls, and now a vast caravan settlement, with boats, car parks and a pleasing Georgian pub. Forthampton Court lies not far from Lower Lode and once belonged to Tewkesbury Abbey. Its fourteenth century Great Hall, to which the last abbot retired, retains its mediaeval roof and adjoining chapel.

The parish church, a large heavily restored one, stands high above the valley, a marvellous viewpoint looking down towards Gloucester. Its walls escaped scraping, the great stone altar with its consecration crosses is still in place, there are the Royal Arms of George III painted on metal, and a monument to John Rastell, who died in 1631, which has a skeleton carved at the bottom. The Victorian bell-ringers' rules in the tower, signed by the curate, the wardens and a magistrate, prohibit the old custom of asking the parishioners for drink at Christmas; while outside the lychgate are whipping-post and stocks, still fairly intact in spite of being declared in 1620, "so insufficient that they would not hold a rogue."

Some fine trees have survived in the grounds of the Court, although Samuel Rudder deplored the damage being done to the splendid oaks by parishioners whose conduct, he thought, doubly inexcusable because of the amount of cheap coal available. Not only was it brought down by barge, there was also much in the river, and the inhabitants along these banks were said to spend much of their time in the water. They raked it in summer, and stirred and netted it in winter, looking for the small coal lying on the bottom, which they then sold to the Gloucester forges.

A mile below Forthampton, the Severn passes between Chaceley and Deerhurst. The importance of the latter has led to the neglect of the former. Both names indicate the once thickly forested nature of this part of the valley. Chaceley church is large and its Norman chancel arch has a primitive head at the centre. There is a striking south arcade, added in the fourteenth century, with corbels of men with long hair which would not have been out of place in this century. Like Forthampton, the stocks, which would hold three prisoners, have survived; and the wardens seem to have saved themselves expense by using a drum with the Royal Arms of 1817, instead of the usual board.

Deerhurst Church.

Across the Severn, and on the line of the old ferry at Chaceley Stock, stands St Mary's, Deerhurst, one of the great Anglo-Saxon foundations. Although Canute and Edmund Ironside agreed to the division of England on a nearby island in the river, the early years of the monastery were troubled by the raids of Vikings and others. As a result the church contains elements of interest from many of the building transformations that have ensued; a Virgin and Child from the eighth century; a font from the ninth, which after extraordinary adventures elsewhere, has returned home; a tower, built in the tenth century, with an internal east window, which is duplicated only in

Abyssinia, of all places; and an almost unchanged Puritan seating arrangement. It also contains, on the brass memorial to Richard II's Chief Baron of the Exchequer, his wife's dog, Terri, the only fourteenth century hound to be commemorated by name in this way.

The Priory House adjoins the church and once formed one side of the Benedictine cloister. Down the lane towards the river is Odda's Chapel, yet another almost complete Saxon church. It was used as a farmhouse kitchen for many years and was not discovered until the plaster was removed in 1885. Its dedication is recorded on a stone which had been found in the orchard in the seventeenth century and sent to the Ashmolean. It is inscribed: "Earl Odda had this royal hall built and dedicated in honour of the Holy Trinity for the soul of his brother Aelfric which left the body in this place. Bishop Aeldred dedicated it the second of the Ides of April in the reign of King Edward of the English." (April 12th., 1056).

Camden remarked that Deerhurst "lies very low upon the Severn, whereby it sustains great damage when the river overflows." The survival of its two splendid Saxon buildings is a testimonial to the skill of their early builders and the constancy of those who maintained them. Like many English villages, it has been troubled by dragons. This one was beheaded by a labourer called Smith who killed it with an axe while it was sunning itself with its scales raised. He was rewarded with the estate of Walton Hill, and when Atkyns was writing in 1700, the family still owned the house and treasured the axe. The legend may be connected with the animal head in the entrance porch of the church.

A mile downstream, Tirley and Apperley face each other from opposite sides. Apperley, high above the Severn, has a village green, a duck pond, a cross, a sixteenth century hall, and much new building. The church is built in Victorian brick and has a matching row of Strickland tombstones in the churchyard. Their crest was a turkey cock, reputedly because one of the family went to America with the Cabots and brought the birds back with him.

Benefaction board, Tirley church.

The river near Ashleworth.

Tirley was famed for its apple trees, and when John Evelyn travelled this part of the Severn in 1654 he went along "a way thick planted with cider and fruit." St Michael's church was restored in 1894, miraculously without removing a fragment of wall painting over the chancel arch. There is an opulent memorial to "Ye First Maier of the city of Worcest[r]. He dyd August ye 5th 1684 aged about 55," so he was, presumably, the first after the Restoration. Grateful kinsfolk probably erected the baroque tablet to Mary Browne, who died in 1717, "Like Tabitha always employed in doing good and in Dispersing her Bounty all about her, but in more particular manner to her Relatives."

When Rudder was here the church owned an acre of pasture which provided what was known as "tithe grass" which was used to strew the church floor at Whitsun and Trinity. It still possesses a fine chest and a remarkable clock, made by a local wheelwright. It commemorates an officer in the Gloucestershire Regiment who was killed in 1917 and is made from parts of a windlass from the river bank, a bean drill, a ploughshare, a pistol barrel, a spade, a file and other assorted pieces of metal. The slate Benefaction boards record a gift of money in 1735 to provide coats, shoes and stockings for five poor men not on parish relief, the recipients to appear in their new clothes on St Thomas' Day.

The road from Tirley crosses the river by Haw Bridge which has replaced a temporary one built by The Royal Monmouthshire Royal Engineers* in 1959. The army bridge took the place of the old toll bridge, described by Bennet in his *History of Tewkesbury* as "one of the many mementos of the late-speculating era." It had three cast-iron arches and was destroyed during the 1958 flood when a 200-ton ship struck the western span. It brought down the bridge which killed the master of the vessel.

There were wharves here from early times and the household accounts of Bishop Swinfield in 1289 give details of a shipment of five casks of red wine from Bristol. Some of it was unloaded at Haw and the rest at Upton, the servants accompanying it being provided with mats to protect the casks from frost and rain.

The flood plain is over three miles wide, keeping the villages well back from the river. Hasfield on the west side, with the Court and church adjoining, was very much the domain of the Pauncefoot family. The house has a panelled room with Biblical texts and the initials of Richard and Dorothy Pauncefoot. She died in 1568 and her tomb chest is in the sanctuary of the church. Both buildings have been heavily restored, the church by Thomas Fulljames, whose father lived at the Court. The father is buried inside the church, the son out in the churchyard.

Almost due east, across the water meadows and ditches, the parish church of Leigh stands isolated from its village. It belonged to Deerhurst and its embattled tower is decorated with gargoyles and the decapitated figure of St Catherine, huddled in a canopied niche.

Habitation reappears on the bank at Ashleworth Quay with its *Boat Inn*. The tow-path changed sides here, so a ferry was needed. Across the fields behind the pub is a group of mediaeval buildings which is almost as unique as the Saxon settlement at Deerhurst. The Court and the great Tithe Barn, over forty yards long, were both built towards the end of the fifteenth century and have remained virtually unaltered ever since. They are made of limestone, but the Manor House, which dates from the same century, is timber-framed. The buildings look out on the village green and cluster protectively around the church. Out of keeping, out of sight, but splendidly situated to the north, is Foscombe, a Gothic extravaganza, built in 1860 by Thomas Fulljames.

The church has been flooded many times, occasionally above the pews, but the herring-bone masonry in the north wall looks little the worse after nearly nine hundred years existence. The west wall of the south aisle is filled by a huge Royal Arms of Elizabeth I which, presumably, once adorned the rood screen. The furniture is chiefly seventeenth century but there are surprisingly few monuments.

---

*The senior reserve regiment of the British Army, taking precedence after the regular forces. It is unique in being distinguished by two "royals" and traces its origin to the militia regiments which arose from the Elizabethan Trained Bands.

The Tithe Barn, Ashleworth.

The road from Ashleworth ferry leads, on the other side of the river, to Sandhurst, a straggling village which has remained relatively undeveloped because of flooding. The church has a Jacobean pulpit and one of the county's nine Romanesque lead fonts. This is one of six, all cast from the same mould, probably in a flat strip. The pattern consists of an arcade over seated figures, holding books and raising their hands in blessing.

Bigland recorded a monument to Gerald Prior, "faithful Preacher of ye Gospel who in his life time dis/recovered the concealed Vicarage of Sandhurst, built ye house, procured ye Lecture and after 53 years Labor in ye Ministry put off ys Tabernacle and was buryed" in 1654, aged seventy-six. The Benefaction board has the gifts of another seventeenth century philanthropist, Walter Howard, who provided money for a gallery, for bread and wine at the monthly communion, for "a fair silver bowl for the communion service," for Foxe's *Book of Martyrs* in two volumes, as well as £5 towards building the vicarage. The west window in the north aisle has a charming stained glass memorial to the dead of the Second World War, and the churchyard has several fine table tombs.

The river runs uninterrupted down the Long Reach to Maisemore where it divides to enclose Alney Island and so, incidentally, provide a natural double ditch for the western defences of Gloucester. Maisemore (the name probably derives from the Welsh Maes Mawr, the Great Field) has become a Gloucester dormitory, leaving the church and Court isolated at the end of a long straight road. They stand high above the river which is here crossed by a modern bridge.

The embattled church tower has retained its gargoyles, otherwise it was almost entirely rebuilt in the nineteenth century. It contains a Jacobean pulpit complete with hour-glass, and a large, well-preserved Royal Arms of George III. There is a set of hand-bells and in the churchyard a tombstone, more philosophical than most, which includes the lines:

"One week's extremity will teach us more
Than long prosperity has done before."

Maisemore Church.

Gloucester began as Glevum, a Roman outpost in the tribal area of the Dobunni, and by the end of the first century had become a colonia for retired army veterans. The four streets of the fortress met where the four main streets meet today, while beyond the walls, the city spreads down to the quays lining the old course of the river. When the Romans had gone, the Saxons moved in, and in the seventh century it became part of the kingdom of Mercia with a royal palace at Kingsholm. Late in that century, King Osric founded the abbey of St Peter in a corner of the old Roman city. Danish raids were repulsed by Alfred's daughter, Aethelfleda, and when the Normans arrived, it was a prosperous town containing ten churches.

William the First refortified it and appointed Serlo, a thirty-six year-old monk, to be abbot of St Peter's. During his thirty-two years at the Abbey he began a complete rebuilding and raised the number of monks from two to nearly one hundred. His great church was consecrated in 1100 and he died four years later. Although a fire did much damage in 1122, the wealth of the monks allowed building to continue throughout the thirteenth century. Of all the treasures which have survived from those early years, perhaps the famous gold candlestick, now in the Victoria and Albert Museum, is the most remarkable. Only sixteen inches high and made between 1104 and 1113, it depicts nine human beings and forty-two clawing beasts, entwined in scrolls of delicate foliage. It is a miracle of craftsmanship and a witness to the wealth of the Abbey.

The decision to bring the body of the murdered Edward II from Berkeley, and give it honourable burial, brought many new pilgrims to the Cathedral, and their offerings added to the abbey's riches. These in turn made possible the erection of the great east window, designed to be a tribute to the Virgin, and a war memorial to those who fought at Crecy. One hundred years later the tower, with its splendid parapet and pinnacles, was completed. Leland called it, "a Pharos to all partes about from the hilles." The Lady Chapel, later in that century, was the last major addition before Henry VIII converted the Abbey into a Cathedral in 1541.

Meanwhile the town, which had been given a charter of liberties by Henry II, was evolving around its market. Full rights to elect a mayor and hold courts were not granted until 1483, but murage tolls had been collected as early as 1226. Civic pride has always been a characteristic of the city and it was emphasised by the mayor at the outbreak of the Civil War, in which Gloucester played no small part, when he assured the electors that "Each of you, with St. Paul, may say 'I am a citizen of no mean or obscure city.'"

The town's great asset was its position on the lowest point at which the river could be bridged; and there has been one here since the twelfth century or earlier. Bishop Swinfield crossed two in 1226, and when Leland came here he described a succession of them; a seven-arched stone one nearest the town; then one of five arches; followed by "the Greate causey of stone forced up through the low meads of Severne" for a quarter of a mile; and finally a bridge of eight arches, "not yet finished."

Of the two main bridges today, Westgate Bridge was built by Sir Robert Smirke in 1814, and Over Bridge by Telford in 1825. The Reverend F. E. Witts saw the latter under construction; "great heaps of fine stone ready squared in large blocks of different sorts for the foundation and super-structure. A steam engine was erecting and several cranes were in operation, lifting masses of stone from the barges in which they were conveyed." He found the arch remarkable, being made up of "two dissimilar curves worked into one."

The old course of the Severn had silted up by the time Leland was writing, and its quay, along with "divers pretty streets" such as Silver Girdle Street, had been abandoned owing to "the raging flood of Severn." A new quay, "whither picards* and small ships come," was near the castle, but the real beauty of the town lay, he thought, in the two crossing streets which met at "an aqueduct incallated." This was the High Cross, removed in 1751. Torrington probably found the aqueduct when, in 1787, he came across "a most beautiful old conduit . . . which was removed here . . . when the noble old cross was demolished: it is the lightest Gothic sculpture . . . and now serves for a tea or wine drinking house."

Although a few visitors deplored the destruction of the High Cross, the *Gloucester New Guide* was justifying it in 1802, pointing out that the town was much disfigured by irregular buildings which hindered the passage of vehicles. The High Cross, "from its unfortunate situation in the centre of four principal streets, an actual nuisance, (had) with great propriety been taken down." Once this had been done, it was not long before Trinity church tower, a row of houses in Westgate Street, and the four gates, none of which "could balance the inconvenience occasioned by them to the inhabitants," had gone the same way.

Nor did things stop there, and the site of High Cross has been lately transformed into a traffic battlefield, watched by little groups of bewildered pedestrians waiting to cross. In exchange, King's Square has had the traffic excluded, but that cold, concrete expanse, with its restlessly squirting water, is an alien refuge and, certainly, no match for the grace and stillness of the Cathedral nearby. On a recent visit a solitary duck, also presumably visiting, was sitting amongst the empty crisp packets, gazing wistfully at the adjoining Golden Egg Restaurant.

Defoe called Gloucester, "an ancient middling city, tolerably built but not fine." It seems to have lost some of its old provincial quality, and to have abandoned its traditional independence for questionable corporate develop-ment. The inscription which Samuel Rudder noticed on the South Gate is even more appropriate today than it was after the Civil War: "A City assaulted by Man but Saved by God."

---

*Boats of about 15 tons or upwards used on the river Severn (*A Law Dictionary,* 1708).

The Cloisters, Gloucester Cathedral.   *W. A. Call*

Indeed, churches have been more successful at survival than secular buildings: Blackfriars, the most complete Dominican friary in the country; St Mary de Crypt, rebuilt in the late fifteenth century, with its fine chancel, and the sounding board of the pulpit from which George Whitefield, born at the nearby *Bell Inn*, preached his first sermon; St Mary de Lode; the tower of the dismembered St Michael's; the superb Commonwealth communion plate of St John the Baptist; and above all, St Nicholas, with coronet, ball and cockerel on its truncated spire.

The last named has become redundant, but is well maintained by a society of friends. It was always closely linked to the river, as the parish included the quays, and was responsible for the maintenance of Gloucester Bridge. Many aldermen, mayors and master craftsmen are buried here, and the quality of its beautifully restored monuments provides the most immediate impression on entering this enchanting church. Amongst the more elaborate are those to Francis Reeve, Mason, Thomas Whithenbery, Carpenter and Samuel Balldwine, Carver, "whose workes in severall parts (without flattery) speak his praise," and who "finished his course in 1645."

Churches such as these are fitting accompaniments to a cathedral which has survived all assaults to become the glory of the county. Even the great east window, lifting the choir roof twenty feet above that of the nave, and bowed to increase its breadth, has retained the original fourteenth century glass. It shines down on a splendid collection of monuments, ranging from the wooden effigy of the Conqueror's eldest son, Robert, through the marvellous alabaster tomb of Edward II, to the simple modern plaque to Ivor Gurney, poet, musician and chorister.

Robert Curthose was nicknamed by his father on account of his short legs. He was fat, slothful, kind-hearted, and distinguished himself only on the First Crusade. The alert, lithe figure in the Cathedral, with hand on sword as if about to draw it, can bear little resemblance to the Conqueror's indolent son, and can be taken as a good example of the truth of Doctor Johnson's dictum about lapidary inscriptions.

This is not so true of the civic dignitaries, many of whom seem to have been sculpted from life. Indeed, Alderman John Jones, three times mayor and Member of Parliament during the Gunpowder Plot, sat for his monument while still alive and, finding the face too red, had it altered, and died the following day. Similarly Alderman Blackleech, (1639) lying on his back beside his wife, has a look of self-satisfied assurance. He came of an important and successful family which was accustomed to get its way. Chancellor Blackleech, who died in 1616, spent his life fighting to retain his office in the face of opposition from the cathedral authorities, and was eventually accused of occupying the Consistory Court "with a rough and vulgar multitude armed with daggers and missiles as for war."

Tomb of Robert Curthose, Gloucester Cathedral. *W. A. Call*

They were a prolific lot. Alderman Machen, sculpted in his mayoral robes, died in 1614 leaving seven sons and six daughters. He is outnumbered by his contemporary John Bower, with nine sons and seven daughters, and a monument emblazoned with the words, "Vayne Vanytie All is but Vayne. Witnesse Solomon." Both fall well below the productive John Semys, who died in 1540, and whose tomb was in old St John's:

"Here under buried John Semys lieth
Which had two wives; the first Elizabeth
And by her six sons and daughters five;
Then after by Agnes his second wife
Eight sons, seven daughters — good plenty
The number in all of six and twenty."

The women who bore all these children, and often died in the process, are less prominent; but the Lady Chapel is graced by the two married daughters of Miles Smith, one of the translators of the Bible and the bishop who suffered from William Laud's five furious years as Dean. Margery Clent, very devout, kneels opposite her more sophisticated sister, Elizabeth Williams, lying serenely on her side, beautifully dressed, her baby at her elbow. They both died in 1622. Elizabeth Millichamp, on the other hand, who died in 1700, "Shunn'd the tattle of the noisy town/And spent her life in caring for her own

119

. . . Desiring to be good/Not minding to be great." But perhaps the most impressive monument to one who died in childbirth is Flaxman's for Sarah Morley. She died at sea on her way home from India at the age of twenty-nine, a few days after the birth of her seventh child.

Sir George Onesiphorus Paul, the prison reformer is here, reconciling, as his memorial tells us, "humanity with punishment and the prevention of crime with individual reform." His monument was by R. W. Sievier, who also made the statue of Jenner; he was a difficult subject, according to Mr Witts, being "broad, thickset, clumsy and the countenance coarse, though very intelligent when lighted up by the talent within." Other memorials include those to Abraham and Charles Rudhall, Sir Hubert Parry, Miss Beale, of Cheltenham Ladies' College fame, (with lettering by Eric Gill), Richard Raikes, Albert Mansbridge, founder of the Workers' Educational Association, and Eli Dupree who, at the age of seventy-four, in 1741, "was abus'd by death."

Outside the Cathedral, a good deal of the Close is used as a car park. Beyond the Close, Bishop Hooper, with his back to St Mary de Lode, gazes at the West Gate where he was burnt to death. The stretch of wall here contains the remains of the building where Richard II held his Parliament in 1378.

Gloucester Docks.

A few good houses have been retained, but not many in their original state. *The New Inn*, built in mid-fifteenth century by one of the monks, to hold two hundred pilgrims, is externally much the same; internally unrecognisable. Bishop Hooper's Lodging, later a pin factory, is now the Folk Museum. Ladybellegate House, recently well restored, is occupied by the Gloucester Civic Trust, with a display section to encourage craftsmen. And the house of the Tailor of Gloucester is now a Beatrix Potter centre.

Spa Road commemorates Gloucester's attempt to compete with Cheltenham. In emphasising the healthiness of the city, *Hunt's Directory* in 1850 pointed out that "it is a singular fact that the vergers of the Cathedral, so far back as can be traced, lived to an average of eighty years."

Perhaps the most extraordinary Gloucester character was Jemmy Wood, the banker from Westgate Street, who died in 1836 at the age of eighty. He was immensely wealthy and notoriously mean. He was also an alderman whose will caused a protracted dispute between his relatives and the corporation. Stories of his parsimony abound, one of the more improbable coming to light when one of his terrified servants tried to commit suicide by drinking from a bottle he found marked poison, only to discover that this was the way Mr Wood safeguarded his brandy. He is buried in St Mary de Crypt. Statuettes of him, standing with hands deep in his pockets have survived, and the Folk Museum has his cash box on which are carved the names of his unfortunate clerks.

Although Romans, Saxons and Normans developed the quays along the Severn, Gloucester was not chartered as a port until Queen Elizabeth I's time. When Celia Fiennes was here she found it flourishing, fine Warwickshire coal being unloaded from the trows to be dragged through the streets on sledges. The present port includes the enclosed City Dock, the Gloucester and Sharpness Canal, and the Ocean Dock at Sharpness, some sixteen miles south. Mr Witts attended the opening of the canal on 26th April, 1827, when the first beflagged ships arrived at Gloucester, one of them a large three-master. Huge crowds enjoyed the celebrations, though even larger numbers assembled two days later to watch the execution of the brothers Dyer.

There is a grand eighteenth century Customs House, a Mariners' Chapel with "The Canal for Christ" embroidered on a screen, and some good warehouses around the dock. Gloucester's other canal, to the Wye at Hereford, had a less happy history. It was begun with high enthusiasm in 1798 but then took forty-seven years to complete, being opened just in time to be replaced by the railway. In contrast to the excitement and crowds at the opening of the Sharpness Canal, there were no official celebrations and not a single person came to watch the final operations.

CHAPTER FIVE

Gloucester to Beachley

THE two arms of the Severn reunite at Lower Parting. On the east bank are the depressing remains of Llanthony Secunda, that twelfth century refuge of monks from a remote valley in Monmouthshire. Being closer to the fleshpots of Gloucester, they soon outstripped in wealth and possessions their sturdier country cousins. Yet today the bedraggled relics of Llanthony Secunda compare sadly with the marvellous priory, still standing in the Black Mountains from which they fled.

The Gloucester house, closely linked with the castle provided hospitality for important visitors, including Edward II who spent Palm Sunday here on the way to his death at Berkeley in 1327. The monks owned many fisheries in the Severn and much farmland, but the only evidence of grandeur left is a ruined tithe barn, a gateway and a timber-framed house. Mr Witts visited it when the Sharpness Canal was being widened in 1847, and was told of ancient sewers, stone coffins and masonry being frequently laid bare by the workmen.

The monks were famous for their cheese, and both Leland and Rudder commended the meadows around here for the quality of their produce. William Marshall, on the other hand, thought Gloucester cheese overrated because it was coloured by a secret West Indian drug, prepared in London. This had first been done, he thought, for fraudulent reasons, but when the practice was copied by other cheesemakers, it was assumed that the colour was important, and it became difficult to sell any that had not been treated.

The road from the docks rises to the church of St Swithun at Hempsted. It lies deep in the heart of Gloucester's suburbs, but high above the river, with pleasing views westward to Highnam steeple. The church was rebuilt, late in the fifteenth century by a prior, Henry Dene, of Llanthony Secunda who later became Archbishop of Canterbury. The mitred head on one of the corbels in the painted nave roof may have been intended to represent him. The interior is whitewashed and has memorials to the Lysons and the Atkyns, two families whose members did much for the study of antiquity in Gloucestershire. The large churchyard contains the table tomb of a Cavalier officer who was killed at the siege of Gloucester in 1643. It is inscribed "Scloptariae glandis ictu trajectus," and there is a legend that the King attended the funeral.

The Gates of Elmore Court.

From Hempsted the straight line of the canal is in sharp contrast with the constantly meandering river. At Stonebench, not something to sit on, but a shelf of rock extending threequarters of the way across the Severn, the two come very close. The river then turns north to begin a long half-turn to Longney before changing course again to encircle Arlingham. The countryside is flat and is not enhanced by the pylons which litter it, nor is the river improved by the concrete and distasteful rubble with which the banks are strengthened.

But there are redeeming villages, and Elmore is one of them. It is very long, with the houses set well back from the wide grass verges, and with the splendid gates of Elmore Court as the focal point. The house, for many years the home of the Guise family, is Elizabethan and has gilded chimney-pieces and a fine staircase. The family produced many soldiers, orientalists and connoisseurs, some of them buried in the parish church.

This is more than a mile from the village and is notable for the collection of table tombs in the churchyard. Carved in high relief, with mourners, skulls, reapers, corpses, hour-glasses and the like, they bear witness to a fine tradition of craftsmanship which has influenced the whole neighbourhood. The upright headstones are equally carefully carved and the inscriptions more imaginative than is usual: "She lived in love and died in peace," for example, happily commemorating the appropriately named Comfort Watts.

The attractive Early English interior contains many Guise memorials. They range from the simple tomb chest of Johannes and Alicia Gyse of 1472 to the elaborately twisted columns and gilded detail of Sir William in 1653. The tablet to General Sir John Guise, who died in 1895, is in the shape of a Victoria Cross and inscribed "16 and 17 Nov. 1857 For Valour."

This was the second relief of Lucknow and the storming of the Secundra Bagh which was led by Captain Guise. The citation was for gallant conduct "in saving the life of Captain Irby, warding off with his firelock a tulwar-cut made at his head by a sepoy, and in going out under heavy fire to help two wounded men. Also for general gallant conduct throughout the operations for the Relief of the Lucknow garrison. Elected by the officers of the regiment." Those officers included Captain (later Field Marshall) Wolseley. Two other men in the 90th received Victoria Crosses in the same engagement, Sergeant Hill elected by the officers, and Private Graham elected by other privates.

The river turns westward between Elmore Back and Minsterworth where, at low tide, vessels could only pass singly because of Church Rock. There was a ferry here, serving a community closely linked to the river trade, and very much afflicted by flooding. The church, appropriately dedicated to St Peter, was rebuilt in 1870, "retaining the best features of the old." It cost £4,000 and the largest subscriber was, "by profession and preference, not a member of the church of England but a Non-Conformist." Part of a sixteenth century cope is attached to the north wall of the nave and the thirteen carvings on the outside of the building include such unlikely bed-fellows as John Wycliffe, Queen Victoria, Caroline of Ansbach, Bishop Hooper, St Peter and a hippopotamus.

The parson, in Elizabethan times, was entitled to the tithe of fish caught in the pools of the Severn, hardly an easy tithe to collect, and Minsterworth was one of several river parishes endowed with "Lamplande", the profits of which were for the maintenance of lamps in the church. Tirley, Tidenham and Longney were others, while lighting at Ashleworth depended somewhat precariously on a cow and a heifer.

Once again the river turns south towards Longney where it widens before being constricted again near Epney, famous for its Elver Station. It is an establishment originating in *The Anchor Inn* which was used as a packing depot for the export of live elvers to stock the German rivers, four million being sent in 1908 alone. The Germans were still using the place in 1939 but it was eventually taken over by the Ministry of Agriculture.

Rudder described Longney as entirely destitute of antiquities but recommended its superb cider, made from the Longney Russet. He also commented on the cultivation of teazle for the clothing industry and on the amount of celery growing in the hedgerows. The church has a fine porch and several table tombs similar to those at Elmore. The nave has remained unscraped, and the absence of stained glass makes the building beautifully light. There are some mediaeval tiles in the chancel and lists of bell-ringing achievements in the tower. A previous vicar, who died in 1713, is remembered as "Pious, Painful and Profitable in his Office."

The Severn here forms the eastern boundary of the Forest of Dean, a remarkable area of independent people and curious place-names. It was inhabited, according to Mr Witts, writing somewhat enviously, by "a simple, secluded people, who enjoy real and peculiar advantages in a regular demand for their labour, and the absence of all local taxation, the Dean Forest being wholly extra-parochial." This was a paradise which was largely imaginary and was not to last.

At Framilode the river turns west to begin a nine mile circuit which will bring it back to within a mile of where it started. Framilode takes its name from the River Frome which enters the Severn here, along with the Stroudwater Canal. The purpose of the canal was to transport coal to the clothiers of the Stroud valley and it was completed in 1779. Ten years later the Thames and the Severn were linked by an extension of the canal through the Sapperton tunnel to Inglesham. And in July 1800, a Coalbrookdale barge owner made the four hundred mile journey by water, taking fourteen days in all.

It was in the lock-keeper's house at Framilode that Ivor Gurney grew up to love the Gloucestershire countryside in the years before the First World War. His poems are full of affection for this flat and somewhat desolate landscape.

"And who loves joy as he
That dwells in shadows?
Do not forget me quite
O Severn meadows."

Framilode Mill began as a corn mill which was converted into a tinplate works in the eighteenth century, when it was notable for experimenting with new ways of rolling and cutting. Today only the mill pond remains. The church and its matching Victorian vicarage stand on the river's edge, and both are unequal to their setting.

The Severn widens again near Westbury, revealing at low tide great stretches of sand and mud, cut here and there by once navigable channels. Rudder referred to two churches in the churchyard at Westbury, the newer one having been built in 1530. It is difficult to understand this, and the problem is compounded by an inscription in the south aisle window, "This church, built A.D. 1530 was dedicated to the Virgin Mary." The present church is dedicated to St Peter and St Paul and the inscription probably refers to the reconstruction of the south aisle and porch at that time.

One still gets the impression of two churches, the detached tower being nearly twenty yards from the main building. The spire was damaged in 1662 and re-shingled with the cut-up staves of old cider casks. It was repaired again in 1937 with 60,000 new shingles and 100,000 copper nails, all supported on a cradle of magnificent Forest oaks, soaring to a height of 160 feet.

The church contains a font with the date 1583 and the arms of Elizabeth I carved upon it; tablets to the Colchester family; a memorial to Thomas Sinderby, decorated with violin and music album by John Pearce of Frampton; and a host of good Forest gravestones in the churchyard. There is also a copy of Foxe's *Book of Martyrs*, given by a London bookseller in memory of James Baynham, the son of the lord of the manor of Westbury, who was accused of heresy, tortured, and eventually burnt at Newgate in 1532. According to Foxe, when the fire had half consumed him, he called out, "I feel no more pain than if I were on a bed of down; it is to me as a bed of roses."

Next to the church are the gardens of Westbury Court. They were created by Maynard Colchester around 1700, at a time when it was fashionable to own a Dutch water garden. His Elizabethan mansion has gone but his gardens have been rescued by the National Trust. The pavilion, summer house and canals have been restored, and the gardens planted with flowers, shrubs and fruit that would have been available in 1700. It is now an exceptional survival, not only in this country, but even in Holland.

The Summer House and Church spire of Westbury.

The Severn narrows again between Newnham and Arlingham, once an important ferry and crossing-place for the great droves of Welsh cattle, moving along the Welsh Way to Frampton and their destination in the grazing grounds around London. The ferry is mentioned in 1238 when the King granted an oak to the woman keeping the passage at Newnham so that she could build a boat. Rudder maintained that those who knew the river could ride and even drive carriages over the ford at low water. He adds, however, the caution that "some have miscarried."

Newnham is a charming town with a long main street in which pedestrians play second fiddle to the through traffic. Yet many of the quiet lanes leading down to the river are delightful, and its position, with the Forest on one side and the Severn on the other, is superb.

It was a borough in 1187, the only one in the county west of the river. Its fearsome ceremonial sword, now in the Gloucester Museum, is inscribed on the blade: "John Morse beeing Maier this sord did Repaier 1594." Tradition maintains that it was given by King John, a monarch who spent much time hunting in the Forest and figures prominently in local folk-lore, but it is probably from the fifteenth or sixteenth century. The Town Hall is an unassuming nineteenth century building, and there is a pleasant Victorian clock-tower. Good buildings, testifying to the town's earlier prosperity, include Wilcox House, Kingston House and Unlawater House.*

That prosperity depended on the river trade and ship building, with temporary innovations such as a verdigris factory and a seventeenth century glassworks. The latter, reputedly the first to use coal as a fuel, is credited by Murray's *Handbook of 1872* with producing one of the earliest glasshouses in England. Several houses in Church Street and down on the Quay are partly built with blocks of refuse from that industry. Newnham has one other claim to fame as an innovator, the introduction in 1764 of a direct service to London by brigs of 180 tons. A normal voyage took about a fortnight, and the trade flourished in the last quarter of the eighteenth century before succumbing to competition from the canals. The town then returned to its most useful and consistent function, the provision of a market for a wide area of the Forest.

It did this, in spite of the appalling road conditions which persisted since Leland had complained of his journey from Gloucester, "through much low ground, subjecte to al sodeyne rysinges of Severne: so much that after reignes it is very foule to travaile in." He was relieved to find Newnham, "an uplandishe townlet." By the time Arthur Young came this way, it was supposed to be a turnpike, but he found the stones so sharp that they cut his horse's feet to ribbons, and so narrow that his chaise could barely get through. It was as bad across the river, where Marshall in 1789 found the deep ditches on either side so full of water that the roads were like quagmires.

*It was once the home of Walburga, Lady Paget who was entrusted by Queen Victoria with finding a suitable wife for the Prince of Wales. She found him Princess Alexandra of Denmark.

The river from Newnham churchyard.

The highest point in Newnham is occupied by the parish church. It was begun in 1380, replacing an earlier building called The King's Chapel on The Nab. This was much nearer the river, where the banks were subject to undercutting by the strength of the water. The new church suffered during the Civil War, was largely rebuilt in 1874, destroyed by fire in 1881, and built again in the same year. The reredos was paid for by the parishioners at the rate of threepence a ball flower.*

A few remnants from the earlier church remain: a damaged Norman tympanum showing the Tree of Life, and an arcaded Romanesque font with the figures of the Apostles. There is a similar font in Hereford Cathedral and a replica at Mitcheldean. There is also the hatchment of Lady Davy. She came from outside the town and married Sir Humphrey Davy, the inventor of the safety lamp. She died in 1855, and this hatchment from her London house is emblazoned with a flame surrounded by a chain. In the Forest coalpits, long after the lamp had been invented, the free miners continued to find their way by a candle in the end of a clay pipe, gripped between the teeth.

*A decoration of the fourteenth century consisting of a three-petalled bud. It remained popular longer in cider-making districts such as this, as it was thought to represent an apple bud.

The churchyard, with fine views over the Severn, contains many traditional Forest tombstones. Amongst the mariners lying here is one who served under Rodney on "the glorious 12th of April, 1752." There are also two friends who died in a collision between boats in August, 1848:

"Four youthful friends that fated boat contained,
But two alone in life the shore regained."

Half a mile south of Newnham is Bullo Pill, a tidal creek which was first used for boat-building. It was then developed by the Forest of Dean Tramroad, (and later the G.W.R.) as a coal port with wharves, locks and loading shoots. At its busiest it was handling 20,000 tons of Forest coal a year.

Arlingham stands about a mile back from the river-crossing at Newnham, and is reached by a typical, forty yards wide, drove road. It is a pleasant cruciform village with good brick houses and a whitewashed pub at its centre. The church lies a little to the south, surrounded by a multitude of gravestones. It is basically a fourteenth century building with glass of that period in the north windows of the nave. There are two elegant chandeliers and a curious pedestalled almsbox.

The wall monuments include several to the Yate family, one of the more elaborate by Nollekens. John Yate, who endowed the free school which his father had built, is described on his monument as one in whom "The Scholar . . . accomplished the Gentleman as the Christian perfected the Man." Indeed, many of the inscriptions have a nostalgic emphasis on gentility, not least that of Priscilla Bromwich, who died in 1855, "graced by the correct manners of the Old School."

Rudder thought Arlingham the most unhealthy of places owing to the vapours rising from the river. Certainly it has curious links with the Earl of Leicester's Hospital at Warwick, being one of four towns which are entitled to send their poor to that institution. As well as the climate, there were the usual dangers on the river, and the registers record an incident when seventeen soldiers were drowned against the Hockerill, "being cast away in a little oar boate, and overturned by the violence of the waves of the flowing tide." A more unusual accident occurred in 1763 when Stephen Addridge put a flat fish between his teeth when he took it out of the net, "whereupon it twisted into his throat and killed him in two minutes." The vicar put all this down in the register, "as a warning to others, to prevent the like accident."

In 1805, the Board of Agriculture reported on the number of walnut trees in Arlingham parish. "So abundant, indeed, is the fruit this year that it is become an article of commerce, and two vessels are now (October 11th.) being laden with walnuts for Scotland . . . Even at (4/- or 5/- a thousand) the produce of a tree is highly valuable, as 20,000 are not considered an extravagant calculation for a large tree." They are not an obvious feature today, and probably suffered, as did most other walnut trees, from the demand for their timber for use in guns, musket stocks etc. during the Napoleonic Wars.

Fretherne, about two miles downstream, was considered even more unhealthy than Arlingham, many of the villagers, according to Rudder, suffering from ague. David Verey has called St Mary's church "a small Victorian masterpiece." Basil Clarke, on the other hand, described it as "the worst type of village church, grossly over-ornamented and badly designed . . . The exterior is prickly . . . the interior is a Gothic muddle. Nothing is spared us." It was built in 1847 by Francis Niblett for Sir W. L. Darell who provided unlimited funds for the tall crocketed spire, painted and gilded roof timbers, Royal Arms, elaborate clock and churchyard lamp posts. Whether one considers it a muddle or a masterpiece, there is no doubt about its impact.

The sister church at Saul was rebuilt about ten years later. The reredos was imported from St Michael's, Gloucester and is Victorian, like the Jubilee clock. Most of the remains of the earlier church have disappeared, but there are good table tombs in the churchyard, and the pulpit is inscribed "Edmond Beerd John Moren 1636." The village has pleasing nineteenth century terraces amongst the modern in-filling, one of the houses being decorated with carved and painted sailors and doves. Just outside Fretherne, the Stroudwater Canal crossed the Sharpness by an ingenious system of locks which raised it to the same level.

The river now trebles in width between Awre and Frampton, and Rudder, rightly, called the latter "one of the handsomest and pleasantest villages in the county." Although he complained that bricks were getting too expensive, having risen from 6/6 to 8/- per thousand, this is a village of admirable brick building. It has legendary associations with Fair Rosamund, who is said to have been born at the Manor House which belonged to her father. It was named as a borough in 1308, and the fair which was granted two years later eventually became Frampton Feast.

There are many attractive houses around the huge green and down the long road leading to the church, the most important being Frampton Court. It was built in 1733 and has a delightful Gothic orangery at the end of a canal. There is another small green, complete with wayside cross, near the church which is sheltered from the river by the embankment of the Sharpness Canal. Before the canal was built, a tidal creek brought shipping from the river almost to the churchyard walls.

St Mary's was consecrated in 1315 and extensively restored in Victorian times. The lead font is like the one at Sandhurst, and the pulpit has a similar inscription to that at Saul: "William Knight William Shering Church Men 1622." The tower is also inscribed with the initials of church men, "R. W. S. I. 1734." There is a Clifford chapel, Clifford glass, Clifford hatchment and

Clifford tombs, while the vestry has a large stone dedicated to the family "at the proper charge of William Watson Gentleman 1526." As well as monuments to these lords of the manor, there are others to the Clutterbucks of Frampton Court, and to lesser mortals like James Pearce, "Accomptant and Professor of Music," whose marble memorial was erected by his brother John, "Statuary and Diagraphist." John's work can often be recognised by drooping sheaves of foliage. He was almost certainly responsible for the tomb of William Keyes, an harmonious blacksmith, whose monument in the churchyard is carved with music album, violin, bow, bassoon, French horn and flageolet.

Splatt Bridge and the Keeper's house on the Gloucester Canal at Frampton.

The Royal Arms are those of Charles II, there is a splendid chandelier presented to the church in 1756, and a grand chest given in memory of a local doctor "whose embroidery and gifts adorn this church." Its most valuable possession was a pure gold chalice and paten acquired in 1838. One thousand pounds was bequeathed to buy it, but security proved such a nightmare that after thirty years, "agreeable to the vestry vote," it was sold for £605: 5: 0.

Fromebridge Mill, to the east of the village, has a long and distinguished history. It was a corn mill in 1086, then a fulling mill, then a corn mill again until 1760, when it was converted into one of the most important wire works in the country. It made, amongst other things, carding wire, and fish hooks for the Newfoundland fishing fleet. It reverted to being a corn mill in the nineteenth century and still retains its majestic waterwheel. To the west of the village the Sharpness Canal is crossed by Splatt Bridge, which is guarded by one of Robert Mylne's pleasant classical keeper's houses.

The Severn is almost at its widest here, and attempts to reclaim land from it have been frequent. When the Earl of Hereford gave the church at Awre to Monmouth Priory in memory of his father, Milo FitzWalter, in the middle of the twelfth century, he included land called Hayward, which had been regained from the river and embanked. Across the river, six centuries later, the Earl of Berkeley was building a great bulwark, called Hock Crib, near Frampton, and another near "to what is called The New Grounds, inferior to none in England for the richness of its soil." The New Grounds are now within the territory of the Severn Wildfowl Trust.

Awre, on the west bank, is half surrounded by water, like Arlingham on the east. It is a remote community, centred on its noble church and pub, and surrounded by isolated and often ancient houses. It has always been involved with the river, and many times at its mercy. As early as 1362, the fishery which was recorded in the Domesday Survey, was found to be useless, "because the weirs which were built up on it have been broken down by the ebb and flow of the sea and by floods."

It is a recurring theme, and the parish registers refer to many river tragedies. In 1731, for instance, an entry records how the Newnham trow struck upon the sands above Amity Crib, the owner and seventeen passengers drowning, and only four escaping in a small boat. Others are remembered on their gravestones. The Barrett family seem to have been particularly unlucky. Benjamin and Rebecca lost two sons, "Mariners both, Drowned in the River Severn," one in 1796 and the other in 1803.

One of the features of the parish is the number of gravestones, not only in the churchyard, but in the church itself which is almost completely paved in ledger stones. The building is mainly of the thirteenth century, although there was a church here at the time of Domesday. It is high, wide and light and has retained its plaster. There is a sixteenth century screen and a reredos of 1892, put up in honour of the fifteen year-old son of a vicar, with the inscription, "This carving . . . was executed as a labour of love by Miss Violette Cotton and Miss Evelyn Chambers." The tower has recently been shut off from the nave by richly etched glass doors. It encloses the Awre Mortuary, a vast dug-out chest, reputed to have been used to harbour the bodies of the drowned when recovered from the river.

A high peak in the church's history is mentioned in a register in 1759: "Let it be remembered for the honour of the parish . . . that from it first sounded the Psalms of David in English Metre." The metrical psalms were the work of Thomas Sternhold from Blakeney, two miles away, and John Hopkins who may, or may not, have come from Awre. The earliest version of what was to become one of the most widely used books ever published was dedicated to Edward VI, and the British Museum holds more than six hundred editions.

A putcher weir at Awre (1980).

As Awre and Frampton face one another, so do Blakeney and Slimbridge. Blakeney is an agreeable village with a well-kept Victorian church, a Baptist chapel, an Independent chapel, several pubs, and down the maze of lanes to the river, Hagloe House: the Hagloe Crab was one of the great cider apples. Marshall thought that the limestone soils of the Forest were more suitable for Stire cider, the Hagloe coming next in esteem. He had a poor opinion of the much praised Redstreak, calling it "crooked, reclining, ragged and unsightly," and he bewailed the fact that, already in 1789, so many of the famous old cider apples had disappeared.

Further south is the settlement of Gatcombe, containing a house where Sir Francis Drake is said to have stayed when visiting Sir William Winter at Lydney. It looks across the river to the New Grounds which Rudder found invaluable for fattening cattle and which now fatten the geese protected by the Severn Wildfowl Trust. Rudder commented on the true Samphire growing here; it is now a carefully controlled tourist attraction and a research centre of considerable importance.

Early guide books have little to say on Slimbridge except for lengthy details about a family which for many generations produced children with five fingers and a thumb on each hand. It is a peaceful, open village, dominated by the handsome spire of the parish church. It has had pecuniary links with Magdalen College, Oxford since the fifteenth century, thanks to a bequest of £10 annually, from the income of the vicarage, so that Henry VII might be commemorated with a Mass and the singing of the Eucharistic hymn from the top of Magdalen tower.

The interior of the church has beautiful nave arcades with foliated capitals; the two-storied porch is decorated with ball-flower ornament; the lead font is dated 1664; and the west end has a screen, erected in 1914, in memory of William Tyndale, who spent his early days here, and whose brother was buried in the churchyard in 1546. The rector at that time was Owen Oglethorpe, the man who, twelve years later as bishop of Carlisle, crowned Queen Elizabeth in Westminster Abbey. According to Atkyns the west end also commemorated the tempest of the 27th of November, 1703.

There are several good memorials; one, to Drusilla Richens who died in 1805, has a pelican feeding her young; and high on the nave wall is a tablet to Robert and Elizabeth Awood. He was "Practitioner of Physick" at Frampton, and Elizabeth was his daughter.

Sharpness Docks.

The river narrows again as The Royal Drift is turned by Tites Point and Purton East, where the canal nears the river, before the last stretch down to Sharpness. Purton has another of Robert Mylne's delightful canal houses, and faces Purton West on the opposite bank. Between 1875 and 1879, almost exactly one hundred years after the building of the Iron Bridge, the Severn and Wye Railway Company bridged the river here. The contractors used Purton Manor Farm, where Sir Walter Raleigh is reputed to have stayed, as an office.

The bridge carried a line from Berkeley over the Severn, before tunnelling its way south to Lydney. In fog, on 25th October, 1960, it was struck by two oil barges which had been swept up from Sharpness by the flood tide. A pier and two spans fell onto the boats which caught fire. Five men died and the bridge was then demolished. Three arches of a viaduct are the only remains of the Purton Steam Carriage Road, a much earlier attempt to experiment, unsuccessfully as it happened, with railways in the Forest.

Sharpness lies just over a mile downstream from Purton. It is a town which owes its existence to the fact that the canal finishes there, rather than at Berkeley Pill as was first intended. Telford played a part in its construction and probably designed the old entrance lock. The company received Government loans in return for employing Napoleonic War veterans on its construction, and it was opened in 1827. Sharpness became so successful that new locks were built in 1874, along with a company village of shops, offices, school and terraced housing. There are several fine warehouses, and it is still one of the busiest ports on the Severn, being capable of accommodating vessels of 7,000 tons, while ships of 750 tons can continue up the canal to Gloucester.

It faces an older rival in Lydney, which has been of importance since the Iron Age when a hill fort was constructed in what is now Lydney Park. The Romans built within its ramparts, and in the fourth century a temple to the god Nodens was erected, together with accommodation for pilgrims. This Celtic water god has affinity with the Irish Nuad of the Silver Hand, and a carving makes him, appropriately, look like Neptune. Amongst other finds in this area was a superb Romano-British bronze of a wolfhound, possibly the hunting dog which Strabo instances as an important British export. Wolves continued to be a menace in the Forest for many centuries, the vicar of Tidenham, in 1445, being allowed to resign his office because of the danger from them. Other Celtic and Roman artefacts from these sites are in Lydney Park and Gloucester Museum. Their importance was recognised in the nineteenth century when the site was being optimistically referred to as "the Silurian Pompeii."

The Reverend F. E. Witts called Lydney, in 1836, "a large village without pretensions to neatness, or in any way striking." The description still serves; it is a functional town with a long industrial and commercial history which has suffered from the many changes in the means of communication. It has even been affected by the course of the Severn which, until the seventeenth century, permitted ships to reach wharves quite close to the church. A change then made it necessary to develop a port much nearer the river. The work was undertaken by the ironmasters, Pidcock and Humphrey, who cut a canal to Lydney Pill. Once a tidal basin had been created and a tramroad opened, Lydney became the chief Forest port. Some old offices and warehouses remain, while out on the mud flats, the rotting hulks of trows, barges and Nova Scotia schooners commemorate its former glories.

Apart from Lydney Park, a late Victorian mansion, the town has few notable houses; but close to the river beyond the golf course, lies Naas House, the home of a merchant family which included the founder of important charities in Monmouth and Newland. The house is still almost as it was when built in the sixteenth century with a very fine staircase. Lydney, like Slimbridge, had its New Grounds covering about one thousand acres which, in Rudder's time, grew such luxuriant vegetation that cattle were brought from great distances to pasture there.

The church is large and has a spire to rival that at Slimbridge. There is a notable arcaded nave and a good waggon roof. The Royal Arms are those of William and Mary, and there are a hatchment and banner of Lord Bledisloe. The Bathurst Chapel has a number of family memorials, one to Thomas, who died in 1791, and who, "from natural Disposition, preferring the ease of a Retired Life to the Bustle of the World, Passed the greater part of his time in this place of which he was lord of the Manor." Certainly, a most fortunate man. As usual, the churchyard overflows with admirable Forest tombstones.*

Across the river, Berkeley Pill leads to the most impressive group of buildings below Gloucester; the castle, church and town of Berkeley. The site of a Saxon abbey, and a town with its own pre-Conquest mint, it became important when Roger de Dursley adopted the name of Berkeley and took over the castle which had been built in the year after Hastings. The building here today is, in essence, the castle which was remodelled in the decades after Edward II had been brutally murdered within its walls.

John Trevisa became vicar of Berkeley a few years later, and translated Higden's *Polychronicon*, which gave the circumstances and method of the King's murder. The ceiling of the old castle chapel is adorned with verses from Trevisa's translation of the Book of Revelation.

The castle stands next to the church and a little below it. The detached tower, which was rebuilt in 1753, was originally part of the defensive system, the body of the church lying closer to the castle. It was heavily restored by Scott in 1866, though the doom over the chancel arch and the Tudor rose of

---

*These are remarkable for the originality of much of the decoration, the high standard of the carving and the pleasant colour of the stone.

Lydney Docks.

Edward VI were spared on the walls. The thirteenth century arcaded nave, the high chancel arch, and its beautiful stone screen were also allowed to remain and are still the chief glories of the church.

The east window, with its miracles and medical emblems, was refashioned in 1843 as a memorial to Edward Jenner, "the great physician of the human race," whose cottage lies just beyond the north gate of the churchyard. Jenner, whose father was vicar here, was famous, not only for the development of cowpox vaccination, but as a naturalist, geologist, balloonist, botanist, poet and dilettante musician. He used to visit his patients in blue coat, top boots and silver spurs, and incidents in his life are depicted on the kneelers in the clergy stalls.

The principal tombs are inevitably those of the Berkeley family and include Thomas, who was custodian of the castle when the King was murdered. He fought at Crecy and died in 1361. He lies with his wife Katherine, their long hands taut in prayer. Other members of the family are in the mortuary chapel.

Lesser mortals are out in the churchyard. They include Ursula Orchard who seems to have composed her own bitter epitaph:

"Farewell affliction, grief and pain,
Welcome eternal bliss.
Thank God I ne'er shall live again
In such a world as this."

The shore at Lydney.

Leland described Berkeley as "a Market towne haveing a maior and Privilegis . . . no great thynge, but it standeth well and in a very good soyle." Rudder was equally unenthusiastic about the town's "one street of mean buildings." John Wesley was more impressed, finding all parts of the castle in good repair except the lumber room and the chapel. He particularly admired the roof garden and the noble views from the walls. He was under the impression that it was Richard II who was murdered here, but admired the effigy at Gloucester, "with its open manly countenance, though with a touch of melancholy."

The town is pleasantly Georgian with a wide main street, an appropriate centre for the rich agricultural Vale of Berkeley. It once had its own mediaeval port on the Pill; now it is faced by the uncompromisingly functional buildings of the Nuclear Power Station, while four miles to the south lies the equally severe Oldbury Power Station, built ten years later.

Berkeley has played a part in English history for over a thousand years, and its influence has not been solely insular. In 1619 members of the Berkeley Company landed in Virginia to develop the Berkeley Plantation on the James River. Although many of its members were killed by Indians on Good Friday three years later, others survived and its mansion house went on to produce two presidents, William Henry Harnson (1841) and Benjamin Harrison (1888), of the United States.

138

Berkeley Castle.

The Vale of Berkeley was, according to Marshall, most celebrated for its cheese, Double Gloucester being really Double Berkeley. The double prefix was used because it was made from a mixture of morning and evening milk, one hundred gallons of milk making approximately one hundred pounds of cheese. In the eighteenth century this area was producing nearly 1,200 tons a year.

The flat, sparsely inhabited land to the south is dominated by the aptly named Hill, little more than a church in the grounds of Hill Court, the home of the Fust family. St Michael's, outwardly mediaeval, is internally an eighteenth century family mausoleum, with many informative memorials. The coloured marble tablet to Sir John, who died in 1779, tells us, for instance, that "He was of the middle Stature, of a benign and comely countenance," notwithstanding that he had served as a captain in Cumberland's army "to aid in repressing an unprovok'd Rebellion," namely, the '45. Meanwhile, his wife Phillippa was looking after things at home: "She rescued the innocent from the snare of Seduction," her memorial tells us, "and was chiefly instrumental in securing from a deep scene of villainy the family Estate to its lawful Successors."

The greatest benefactor to the neighbourhood seems to have been Sir Francis who, in 1759, "new modelled and repaired his church and built the Great Sewer at Hill Pill." His memorial proclaims his intentions:

"To Drain the Parish from its during flood,
To model and repair the house of God,
Are patterns good I set to Future Time.
Free Profit yours and Cost and Labour Mine."

The monuments, the resplendently canopied family pew, the three-decker pulpit, and the pleasant sixteenth century seating, hardly prepare one, on leaving the church, for the message inscribed on the floor of the porch: "The World is a Wildernesse."

The river bank between Slimbridge and Littleton was divided between nine pills, different parishes being responsible for repair of the flood banks and being rated according to their acreage. Oldbury-on-Severn dominates this flat countryside, its church on a seemingly artificial mound, looking down on the village and across the pill to the Severn Bridge.

It is dedicated to St Arilda who, according to Leland, was martyred near Thornbury, "by one Muncius a Tiraunt who cut off hir head because she would not consent to lye with him." The building was whitewashed as a guide to shipping, and once had a spire which had to be removed after the great storm of 1703. There was a further disaster when the main body of the church caught fire in 1897; so there is little that is old remaining. Bigland recorded a stone in the churchyard in memory of a boy of fifteen who was shipwrecked on the *Swift* snow on February the 2nd, 1735. His ship was driven from anchor in a violent storm and lodged on a rock within the parish where the captain and two seamen also perished.

The land to the south once belonged to Malmesbury Abbey, and as a result, the church at Littleton is dedicated to St Mary of Malmesbury. Like Oldbury, it was almost completely rebuilt in later Victorian times, but managed to retain some heraldic tiles, a good Elizabethan ledger stone to Thomas Archard, and the Royal Arms of Queen Victoria.

The west bank of this last stretch of the river is followed above the flood plain, by the old Roman road, now heavy with traffic. It is punctuated at regular intervals by the villages of Aylburton, Alvington and Woolaston. St Mary's Aylburton is another Severnside church which, like Oldbury and Littleton, was rebuilt in the nineteenth century. It was on a new site but the font, pulpit and Royal Arms of George III were brought from the old building.

St Andrews, Alvington was restored at about the same time. The stone altar with its crosses seems to have been cut from a larger slab which is carved with a primitive crucifix, the arms of the cross seeming to end in hands. In the sanctuary there is a large stone to "Sr Robert Woodrof Knight and Marye his deare wyfe . . . the Cruel Knife soon cut their threed" in 1602. The heating system has very ornate cast-iron radiators.

Woolaston, less closely affected by the traffic which transfixes Alveston, has another church which was almost completely rebuilt in the nineteenth century. In the process it acquired a screen from Sunderland and a pulpit from Northamptonshire. The churchyard is more representative of the locality, with thickly clustered graves to sturdy Woolaston characters like Elizabeth Woodroffe, who died in 1665, "Zealous to God, to her Husband loyal/To Parent Dutiful, Bewail'd by All."

Warren Silcocks, who died in 1843, is commemorated by the well known:

"My sledge and hammer lie reclin'd,
My bellows too have lost their wind:
My fire's extinct, my forge decay'd
And in the dust my vice is laid.
My coal is spent, my iron gone,
My last nail's driven, my work is done."

The lead font at Sandhurst.   The lead font at Tidenham.

The lead font at Frampton.   The lead font at Slimbridge.

141

There is a similar inscription on a stone of 1872 in Llandrinio churchyard. Woolaston had a Roman villa near a tidal pill where one of the corner towers may have been used as a navigation beacon. A similar villa at Aylburton, also down on the river, incorporated its own wharf.

Tidenham, the last parish before the Wye joins the Severn, has a longer history than most. Its Saxon charters go back to the tenth century and give a detailed picture of a large, carefully organised settlement. The parish embraced four tithings, Stroat, Bishton, Sedbury and Beachley, lying in wide strips between the Severn and the Wye. It possessed over sixty fish weirs on the Severn and over twenty on the Wye, presumably similar constructions to the putts or lines of cone-shaped traps one sees on the river today.

At the Conquest, the manor of Tidenham was let to the Archbishop of Canterbury by the Bishop of Bath, at a rent which included, not river fish, but six porpoises and thirty thousand herrings. The community's other Saxon connection, is the stretch of Offa's Dyke near Sedbury, the only part which approaches the Severn, except for the short section near Welshpool.

St Mary's church has a robust square tower which has long acted as a landmark for Severn mariners. Like so many of the churches in this area it was over-restored in the nineteenth century, but it retained its Romanesque lead font, one of the six with the same pattern. The Benefaction Board contains a bequest of 10/- a year from Mrs Maddocks, "to maintain, uphold and paint the arms on the tomb of her ancestors," something which, in 1979, was still being done.

Down towards Sedbury Park, the home of Eleanor Ormerod, a distinguished entomologist, and a house which was enlarged by Robert Smirke in 1825, the river is constricted by Sedbury cliffs and the Beachley peninsula. It was in the bay here that ships going up river were searched by customs officials; and it was also one end of the Old Passage ferry, a crossing from Aust which goes back to pre-Roman times, and has proved one of the most enduring and important routes between England and Wales. It was a crossing which created fear, frustration and fury to almost all who used it. John Wesley denounced it at some length, as did Defoe, and his description is typical of what most travellers felt. Arriving at "a little dirty village called Aust," he found the sea "so broad, the fame of the Bore of the tide so formidable, . . . the water so rough, and which was worse, the boats to carry over both man and horse . . . so very mean, that in short none of us cared to venture," so they passed on to cross at Gloucester.

Today, the crossing is surmounted, and most of the difficulties overcome, by the Severn Bridge which was designed by Sir Gilbert Roberts in 1966. Like so many of our current engineering achievements, it is something which

Telford had proposed in the early nineteenth century. It is a convenient place to abandon the Severn to the Bristol Channel, and turn aside into its most beautiful tributary, the Wye. It would then be possible to follow that superb river back to Plynlimon, to within a mile of where one set out on the Severn, an unparalleled grand tour of about three hundred and sixty-five miles.

The Severn Bridge.

Bibliography

The River.

Bradley, A. G.: *A Book of the Severn.* (1920) Methuen & Co.

Cope, K.: *The Angling Times Book of the Severn.* (1979) David & Charles.

Harral, T.: *The Picturesque Views on the Severn.* (1824) London.

Jordan, C.: *Severn Enterprise.* (1977) A. H. Stockwell.

Peel, J. H. B.: *Portrait of the Severn.* (1968) Hale.

Randall, J.: *The Severn Valley.* (1862 & 1882). *Guide to the Severn Valley Railway.* (N.D.) John Randall.

Rowbotham, F.: *The Severn Bore.* (1964) David & Charles.

Taylor, J. N.: *Fishing on the Lower Severn.* (N.D.) Gloucester City Museums.

Walker, T. A.: *The Severn Tunnel.* (1891) Kingsmead Reprint 1969.

General.

Atkyns, Sir R.: *The Ancient and Present State of Gloucestershire.* (1712) W. Bowyer for Robert Gosling.

Baxter, Richard: *Autobiography.* (1615-1685) Dent 1974.

Bennet, J.: *The History Of Tewkesbury.* (1830) Tewkesbury.

Bigland, R.: *Historical, Monumental & Geneological Collections relative to the County of Gloucester.* (1791) Gloucester.

Borrow, George: *Wild Wales.* (1854) Dent, Everyman Edition.

Burton, J. P.: *History of Bewdley.* (1883) Bewdley.

Cambrian Traveller's Guide. (1813, 1840) G. Nicholson.

Camden, William: *Britannia.* (1586. Translated by R. Gough, 1789) John Nichols.

Churchyard, Thomas: *The Worthines of Wales.* (1587) Spenser Society facsimile 1871.

Clarke, B. F. L.: *Church Builders of the Nineteenth Century.* (1938) S.P.C.K.

Cobbett, William: *Rural Rides.* (1821-1832) Dent Everyman Edition.

Cooke, G. A.: *Topographical & Statistical Description of the Counties of: Salop, Worcester, Gloucester.* (c. 1800) Brimmer & Co.

Cranage, D. H. S.: *An Architectural Account of the Churches of Shropshire.* (1901-1911) Shropshire Archaeological Society.

Defoe, Daniel: *A Tour through the Whole Island of Great Britain.* (1714-1726) Penguin Books 1971.

Dineley, T.: *An Account of the Official Progress of the Duke of Beaufort through Wales.* (1684) Blades, East & Blades 1888.

Drayton, Michael: *Poly-Olbion.* (1622) John Russell Smith 1876.

Dreghorn, W.: *Geology Explained in the Severn Vale and Cotswolds.* (1967) David & Charles.

Eyton, R.: *The Antiquities of Shropshire.* (1854-1860) London.

Fiennes, Celia: *Journeys.* (1685-1703) Cresset Press 1947.

Freeman, G. J.: *Sketches in Wales.* (1823-1825) Longman.

Fuller, Thomas: *The Worthies of England.* (1662) London.

Habington, Thomas: *A Survey of Worcestershire.* (1586-1646) Worcestershire Historical Society 1895-99.

Haslam, Richard: *Powys. The Buildings of Wales.* (1979) Penguin Books.

Hulbert, C.: *The History and Description of Salop.* (1837) Shrewsbury.

Leland, John: *Itinerary.* (1535-1543) Centaur Press 1964.

Lewis, S.: *A Topographical Dictionary of Wales.* (1842) S. Lewis & Co.

Marshall, W.: *The Rural Economy of Gloucestershire.* (1789, 1796) G. Nicol.

Milward, R. & Robinson, A.: *The Welsh Borders.* (1978) Methuen.

Monmouth, Geoffrey of: *History of the Kings of Britain.* (c. 1136) Dent Everyman Edition.

Nash, T. R.: *Collections for the History of Worcestershire.* (1781-2) R. Gough, London.

Nicholls, H. G.: *The Forest of Dean.* (1858) John Murray.

Noake, J.: *Guide to Worcestershire.* (1868) *The Rambler in Worcestershire.* (1848) Worcester.

Pennant, T.: *A Tour in Wales.* (1770-1774) Printed for Wilkie & Robinson 1810.

Pevsner, N.: *Shropshire.* (*Buildings of England, 1958*) *Worcestershire.* (*Buildings of England, 1968*) Penguin Books.

Phillips, Pauline: *A View of Old Montgomeryshire.* (1977) Christopher Davies, Swansea.

Plymley, J.: *General View of the Agriculture of Shropshire.* (1803) Richard Phillips.

Raistrick, A.: *Dynasty of Ironfounders.* (1953) Longman.

Rolt, L. T. C.: *Thomas Telford.* (1958) Penguin Books.

Roscoe, T.: *Wanderings and Excursions in North Wales.* (1836) Tilt & Simpkin.

Rowley, T.: *The Shropshire Landscape.* (1972) Hodder & Stoughton.

Rudder, S.: *A New History of Gloucestershire.* (1779) Cirencester.

Skrine, H.: *Two Successive Tours through the Whole of Wales.* (1798) Elmsley & Bremner.

Swinfield, Bishop: *Household Roll.* (1289-90) Camden Society 1854.

Sylvester, D.: *The Rural Landscape of the Welsh Borderland.* (1969) Macmillan.

Taylor, John (The Water Poet): *Works.* (1630) Reprinted by the Spenser Society 1868-69.

Torrington, Viscount: *Diaries.* (1781, 1787) Methuen (1934).

Trinder, B.: *The Most Extraordinary District in the World.* (1977) *The Industrial Revolution in Shropshire.* (1973) Phillimore.

Verey, David: *Gloucestershire II.* (*The Buildings of England, 1960*) Penguin Books.

Verey, David & Welander, D.: *Gloucester Cathedral.* (1979) Alan Sutton.

Victoria County History: *Worcestershire.* (1901-1924) O.U.P.

Wesley, John: *Journals.* (1731-1796) Dent Everyman Edition.

Willan, T. S.: *River Navigation in England.* (1950) Frank Cass.

Witts, Rev. F. E.: *The Diary of a Cotswold Parson.* 1783-1854. (Ed. David Verey, 1978) Alan Sutton.

Wyndham, H. P.: *A Tour through Monmouthshire & Wales.* (1774, 1777) E. Easton.

Transactions of The Worcestershire Historical Society, The Worcestershire Archaeological Society, The Shropshire Archaeological Society, The Bristol & Gloucestershire Archaeological Society; and The Montgomeryshire Collections of the Powysland Club.

Index

INDEX